INHERITING LIES

JERRY MITCHELL

Copyright © 2024 Jerry Mitchell

Paperback: 979-8-9887938-4-7
Hardback: 979-8-9905760-0-1
Ebook: 979-8-9905760-1-8

Ordering Information:

Books to Life Marketing Ltd
128 City Road, London, EC1V 2NX, UK

Printed in the United States of America

CONTENTS

INSPIRED OR SACRED?

Is the Bible inspired or is it sacred? The answer is relevant to the way one lives their life. If we consider the Bible to simply be inspired, then we could reduce it to nothing more than a literary work of art. Inspiration comes from many sources. Exactly what inspired Leonardo Da Vinci to paint the Mona Lisa as he did has been the subject of speculation for centuries. Michelangelo depicted David nude, was his inspiration to show a mature muscular David who was fit and ready to be a king?

Songwriters, poets, artist who work in oil, acrylics, watercolors or clay, even jewelry makers and architects all have some type of inspiration for their original work. Everyone who has ever written a book, every schoolchild who has ever grudgingly written a story for an assignment has had some kind of inspiration. As we know some of these inspirations come from the wonderful source many Christians name the Holy Spirit, while other darker works seemingly come from an unholy source. Is it possible that the truly inspirational stories found in the Bible come from the Holy Spirit while other tales of woe often found in the same chapters are inspired by an *unholy spirit*? Are we to believe the writers of the Bible could be inspired by both the Holy and unholy at the same time and retain the continuity needed throughout the Bible?

If an inspirational writing is the foundation we use to trust a divine force to guide our lives, why choose the Bible? After all, there are other nice books which have been written that promote civil societies and loving each other. There are many religions to choose from that suggest people should treat each other with respect and those who don't should face some form of punishment. What we find in the Bible is a perfectly matched combination of instructions to promote civil and societal order with suitable consequences for those who disregard not only civil law but divine law coupled with divine instructions that teach us how to live the way our Creator designed us to live. Someone would need a great amount of faith to consider the Bible as nothing more than an inspired work of literature.

For readers of what is known as the New Testament, we could look to 2 Timothy 3:16 as Paul writes, ***All scripture is given by inspiration of God, and is profitable for doctrine, for reproof, for correction, for instruction in righteousness*** (KJV) Is Paul's intention here to actually suggest the writers of what he considered to be Scripture were only inspired? Digging through the language, culture and history might reveal something different. When Paul or Sha'ul as he would have been known to his contemporaries, writes this letter to Timothy, the gospels of the New Testament were not widely known. In fact none of the New testament was considered scripture until the fourth century, nearly 300 years after the letters were written. Paul's use of the word scripture refers to what he would have known as the Torah, prophets and other writings. Today Christians consider that the Old Testament.

Examining the 2 Timothy 3:16 verse one should check the verbiage to ensure the translation is correct. Most are likely to use a familiar resource for this such as the Strong's Concordance. What can be found is a Greek compound word that is given the Strong's number 2315 along with the definition of God breathed or inspired by God. However if you are able to dig a little deeper what you will discover is the first part of the compound word *Theo* for God and then something amazing *pneustos* (*Greek*) breathing out! Simply stated Paul writes that the Old Testament is the words that God Himself breathed out and gave to the writers to document His desire and His plan. Not inspiration (to take in) but breathed out by the Creator Himself.

Deuteronomy 29:29 reads, ***The secret things belong unto the LORD our God: but those things which are revealed belong unto us and to our children for ever, that we may do all the words of this law.*** What He chooses to give to us He gives and He chooses who will deliver the message. To make this even more dramatic when we look into a Hebrew translation of Paul's letter, the word *Theopneustos* (θεόπνευστος) becomes 2 Hebrew words אלהים ברוח pronounced *baruch elohim* in context it is the breath or spirit of God. Not only are we offered the words of our Creator we are also offered at the same time His spirit within those words. This means the Bible is not simply inspired, it is **sacred**.

The difference between inspired and sacred is as far as east is from west. Sacred is holy, set apart and given respect and reverence. Sacred can only come from the Divine Creator. Someone who is merely inspired to write something can not use the phrase *thus saith the LORD*, as we find throughout the Bible. Any writer who is inspired by another can not speak for or put words into the mouth of the inspirer, especially if the speaker never spoke the words.

Traditions, doctrines and old wives tales have been allowed to pervert the sacred words of our Creator. Sayings such as *cleanliness is next to Godliness,* may be a great way to teach young people to clean up a mess or to wash their hands but it can not be found in the Bible. *Hate the sin and not the sinner* may sound Biblical but it was actually a quote from Mahatma Gandhi[1] who practiced Hinduism all of his life. What we read in the gospel of Matthew that many Christians confuse this with is found in chapter 5:43-44 **Ye have heard that it hath been said, Thou shalt love thy neighbour, and hate thine enemy. But I say unto you, Love your enemies, bless them that curse you, do good to them that hate you, and pray for them which despitefully use you, and persecute you.** (KJV) While the Greek word used here is translated as love, we could translate it as wish well for your enemies or even reason with your enemies and show them respect. Psalm 5 gives us a very different frame of reference in verses 4–5 **For thou art not a God that hath pleasure in wickedness: neither shall evil dwell with thee. The foolish shall not stand in thy sight: thou hatest all workers of iniquity.** (KJV) Here we read that even God hates those who refuse to follow His instructions. Is this a conflict found in the Bible? Absolutely not! This conflict belongs to our understanding and the way we have been taught to think about God and the Bible.

Language has a bad habit of evolving. Only a few years ago the English word cool was defined as a low temperature while today it can mean neat or interesting. When we confuse things even more with translation issues and with

---

[1]   Gandhi: An autobiography by Mahatma Gandhi.

personal emotions, then compound the problem with doctrinal agendas. What we are left with is disfunction. Trying to fit our traditions, doctrines or even our own beliefs into the Bible prevents the words of our Divine Creator from functioning properly to guide our lives. Reading the Bible through the filters of Tradition or even our own denominational doctrines is like trying to view the Beauty of the cosmos through the clouds. We know there is something absolutely breathtaking there but we just can't see it.

Long ago Jeremiah recorded the words of our Creator that were given to him. Through 5 kings Jeremiah spoke and wrote and even lamented. Some of his own words are included as he cries out in warning and for mercy. Jeremiah 16:19 ***O Lord, my strength, and my fortress, and my refuge in the day of affliction, the Gentiles shall come unto thee from the ends of the earth, and shall say, Surely our fathers have inherited lies, vanity, and things wherein there is no profit.*** (KJV) As Jeremiah pours out his soul to his Creator he reveals that in the day of trouble the people will come back to God and say we were lied to. We were told things that had no value, empty lies that were completely worthless. But he didn't stop there, he continued in verse 20 ***Shall a man make gods unto himself, and they are no gods?*** (KJV) In other words, we have been praying to nothing.

Jeremiah's interaction with his Creator gave him more than just a message to deliver, that relationship gave him hope. Jeremiah's trust that there would be some people who would be willing to find the truth, they would hear or read the Creator's words the way He spoke them, to view the stars through cloudless skies. To understand the Words that he and the other prophets delivered on behalf of the Creator of the universe. Every generation has had some who have found that truth and every generation has had many who ridicule and persecute those who choose to follow the Creator's instructions.

Even today there are certain Christian denomination who attempt to force evolution into the lesson of Creation. Some Jewish scientist speak about archaeological evidence of 10,000 years ago. If we truly believe the Bible to be the sacred word or spirit of our Creator given directly to Moses and the prophets, why would we attempt to contradict His authority? Those who try to justify the evolution theory into the lessons we find in Genesis 1 are as guilty as the serpent because they are asking the same question, *Did God really say?* Jeremiah understood there would be those who question God and the warning in his prayer remains overlooked by the arrogant. We have inherited lies, our responsibility is to search through the language, culture and history to find the truth revealed in the words of our Creator.

Hermeneutical interpretation has been applied to the Bible by many people for a long time but can hermeneutics reveal the lessons we are to learn? Interpretation means to explain the meaning of, while hermeneutics is the methodical theory of interpretation. This sounds very scientific but the reality is that there are rules to apply hermeneutics but they are not consistent between the people who use them. Meaning some schools teach how to apply hermeneutics differently from another school. Without consistency all we have is someones best guess. Maybe the old joke used by the the speaker who says in their most authoritative voice, "I have many post graduate degrees including three masters, I don't just guess, I form an *educated* guess."

Without the benefit of cross-referencing each verse and every original word, interpretation, even hermeneutical interpretation fails to provide the absolute, definitive answers because it is only speculation, a guess. There is a difference between reading the Bible, studying the Bible and examining the Bible. If we are reading for enjoyment, comfort, guidance or many other reasons, we can read almost any translation and receive benefit. If we choose to study there are some translations that have more resources associated with them than others. The King James Bible probably has the most accompanying list of materials because it has been around for so long. But when we really want to get to the treasures that are found in the lessons of the Bible, we examine it forensically. Not like a forensic scientist would examine a single physical piece of evidence but as one would examine a crime scene. Searching for all of the clues to find out *who done it.*

Using every resource available including the dictionaries published at approximately the same time a translation was published because language is fluid. Language evolves and changes, slang and figures of speech are used by different cultures differently. Even if you don't speak the language originally used to write the Bible a good concordance is necessary for definition and cross referencing words and verses. Many find an interlinear Bible to be very helpful, and today there are many resources available free on the internet from many sources. A warning here is necessary, be careful when seeking these resources and check their sources. Some people are masquerading to prey on you. These are wolves in sheep's clothing hoping that because you are looking for Biblical material you will be an easy target for them to manipulate into giving them money or much worse. Commentaries are another resource that come with a warning. Commentaries are nothing more than someone writing down what their interpretation is. If ones commentary is nothing more than a parroted paraphrase of another it is less than useless and can be harmful if it leads others away from the truth. Resources are tools and like any craftsman, using quality tools produces quality work, just don't confuse quality with expense. The best quality tool when examining the Bible is completely free. Prayer is the first thing we should consider when approaching the Bible, after all He gives it to us through His spirit and His prophets. Allow The Almighty to guide you and reveal the things He desires you to know. Examining the Bible forensically. Searching for the clues that bind together the places and events written about that are often separated by hundreds of years to find the treasure that is the true word and spirit of our Creator. The Bible has been considered the greatest hyperlinked text ever compiled. That is why cross-referencing is vitally important. Understanding that one character may be quoting someone form their past. Knowing who is speaking to whom helps keep what is being said in context. Having the ability to recognize a transcript of a conversation is different from a monologue. Reading the prophets of old and understanding if what they are writing is God's words or their perspective or even their own prayer. While we are able to benefit greatly from the advice and examples we find in the Bible, it wasn't written directly to us living in the 21st century. We are literally reading someone else's mail, especially the New Testament. The letters of the gospel writers, Paul and the others were written for and addressed to specific groups or individuals. To grasp their instruction we need to know about the people they were writing to. We should search through the Bible to find out if the one writing had actually met with the people or person to whom they were writing. This is especially critical when we think of Paul's letters. Would he need to issue new instructions to a group of people he had lived among for almost 2 years as many propose he did with the Corinthians? Probably not, yet some will read Paul's letters as if he is giving personal instructions directly to us today. Much of his writing is clarification of what is already written somewhere else in the Bible.

The lies and traditions we have inherited have done nothing to bring clarity to the Bible, they only confuse it. Because the Bible is the word and spirit of God and He alone is perfect, the Bible can not contain contradictions. Anything we may consider as contradictory is our own foolishness because we are trying to see the distant galaxies through the clouds. We are trying to interpret what is there by guessing and hoping we are right instead of diligently and rightly dividing the word, being careful not to add to or diminish from what our Creator has spoken. If we think about the difference between what we have been taught and what is really in the Bible, there are things that should be obvious. Nowhere in the Bible can we find *cleanliness is next to Godliness*. We can not find chapter or verse that definitively reads Jesus was born on December 25. *God helps those who help themselves* is another example of something that may sound Biblical but is not. From Enoch magically disappearing to the 3 wise men and beyond, tradition has replaced the true words given from our Creator. Some of these lies seem harmless until we realize how deep the well of lies that we draw from really is, how thick the cloud cover is that we can't see through.

When we begin to read the bible to find what is really there without trying to force our traditions or doctrines to fit where they don't belong, we are not testing God, we are testing ourselves. Some have confessed to have had a crises of faith when faced with what the Bible really reveals. Long established consensus of thought concerning time and events are being reconsidered as new archeological information is unearthed. Recent evidence suggests that Moses may have known the Egyptian Pharaoh Tutankhamen, better known as King Tut. The excavation of Jericho many years ago revealed the Biblical account of Rahab's home being kept safe as the walls came crashing down is accurate and the list continues to grow.

We must be willing to accept that there are things we were trained to think about the Bible that are nothing more than the lies of tradition or denominational doctrine. The responsibility of every generation of believers is to test what we have been taught using the Bible as the true standard of truth. Too often believers have become horrified when they realize they have fallen prey to those who promote their own agenda using Biblical sounding information. Peter Popoff is one of the more famous false faith healers who was allegedly exposed in 1986 for using a hidden earpiece to secretly communicate information about the people in the audience from his wife. Popoff claimed that God revealed the information to him concerning address and illnesses of the people who came to him seeking healing. The prophet Hosea issues a stern warning that is applicable for us today, he begins chapter 4 by saying, ***Hear the word of the LORD***. (KJV) He goes on to write about the people who do not know the truth and finally in verse 6 we read, ***My people are destroyed for lack of knowledge***: (KJV) The warning is for those who have rejected or refused His knowledge however we could extrapolate that to include those who would put their faith in either a person or their false teaching in place of the instructions given to us by the one who designed us.

Everyone wants to believe the information they have received from someone they trust is true. A child should expect a parent to **offer them sound instruction.** After all Solomon wrote in Proverbs 22:6 ***Train up a child in the way he should go: and when he is old, he will not depart from it.*** (KJV) A student should expect a teacher to offer correct instruction as well, and even as adults we should be able to to trust the information we are given by those we choose to love and honor. What happens when the information we have received, information that was offered in good faith, turns out to be incorrect? Even when the one giving the information believed it, that doesn't magically make it truth. Many adults have a strong desire for the fictional Santa Clause to be true and so they pass along the fairy tale as truth to the very young. Lying to a child about a fairy tale doesn't sound harmful. What harm could possibly come from a parent telling a child there is a mysterious man who gives children presents or a giant bunny to give candy or even a little fairy that collects children's teeth in return for money? When they learn the truth, children realize they can not trust their parents. The very people whom they should expect complete security from. The ones who are instructed to train their children in the way they should go are teaching them to expect to be lied to and in return to lie themselves. Then, as the child grows these same parents are upset when the child lies to the parents. This isn't quite so cute and harmless now is it?

Every individual from every generation should be searching to discern fact from fiction, truth from lies, Biblical authority from traditions and disconnected doctrine that has brought humanity itself into conflict with our Creator. Instead of blindly believing information that sounds good or following false prophets, believers should strive to live the way our Creator designed us to live. If we choose to consider the God of Abraham, Isaac and Jacob as our God, we should be excited to learn as much about Him as possible. To know His power and authority, to listen for His voice and do as He instructs us to do. The only way to achieve that is to uncover the lies we have inherited, strip away the meaningless traditions that cloud and confuse and accept that every sacred word He gives to us through His prophets is true. Then we can begin to clear the confusion, recognize our contradictions, discard our doctrines that are contrary to the Bible and view the glory of all His creation through crisp, cloudless skies.

WHO DO YOU CALL GOD?

Every person who attends a church or synagogue does so for their own reason. Some go because they feel they are obligated, some go because they just always have and some, to be part of a group of believers. There are many who attend because they feel a true love for their Creator and desire a stronger, more meaningful relationship with Him. While many people spend their entire lives attending the same house of worship, others will move from place to place. Some remain faithful to the denomination they're first introduced into and some may visit different denominations or even visit a synagogue if they are Christian. No one should question the motivation of someone who is comfortable where they attend any more than they should question the *church hopper.*

Individuals seek the Creator in their own way. Just as Christianity has many different denominations such as Catholic or protestant (and there are an almost unlimited number of Protestant denominations,) Jewish believers also have some differing paths to choose from. Most people are familiar with the orthodox or Ulna-Orthodox but don't realize there are also the Hasidic, reform, Jewish Renewal and

Karaite to name a very few. An older Rabbi was asked (by me) how many different sects or denominations of Judaism are there in the world. His answer was simple, "How many Jews are there in the world?" He went on to explain that our Creator sees us as individuals first and so each of us has the opportunity on an individual basis to know the one who created us as an individual also. If one were to attend a family reunion, the oldest male family member would be considered by some to be a father, grand father and maybe a great grand father. To others he may be an uncle, and yet he is someone's son or possibly even a brother. He is, in this example the living patriarch of the family. He is known to different members of his family differently. That is much the same as we could view our Creator. Some people see God as Father, some as Creator, some as Almighty but He is still the same individual although He has many, many more characteristics.

Moses records the first mention of God in Hebrew as אלהים pronounced Elohim. This is a plural form of His title, not His name. That may seem confusing, however it is really quite easy to grasp this concept. אלהים has many characteristics, He is Father, Creator, Almighty and is also know by other defining identities throughout the Bible. A title is just that it is a job description, Not to belittle אלהים at all, think of a judge being referred to as *Your Honor*. The judge in most instances should be a lawyer also so his title as judge in English although singular, represents many aspects of who the person is and what they may do. In almost every English Bible the Title אלהים is translated as God with a capital *G* when referring to the Creator. This can also be used to refer to the gods with a lower case *g* when it refers to the other gods as in Exodus 20:3 **Thou shalt have no other gods before me.** However one needs to be aware that the name of אלהים God also is used throughout the Hebrew in the Christian old Testament. The four Hebrew letters that make the name of אלהימ are יהוה known as the Tetragrammaton, this is what is most commonly translated as LORD in the English Bibles. This name is of such extreme importance it is used 5, 410 time in the Hebrew Bible (the Christian Old Testament) and each book can be counted this way; Genesis 153 times, Exodus 364, Leviticus 285, Numbers 387, Deuteronomy 230, Joshua 170, Judges 158, Samuel 423, Kings 467, Isaiah 367, Jeremiah 555, Ezekiel 211, Minor Prophets 345, Psalms 645, Proverbs 87, Job 31, Ruth 16, Lamentations 32, Daniel 7, Ezra-Nehemiah 31, Chronicles 446. In Exodus 3:15 we read, ***And God (אלהים) said moreover unto Moses, Thus shalt thou say unto the children of Israel, the LORD (יהוה) God (אלהים) of your fathers, the God of Abraham, the God of Isaac, and the God of Jacob, hath sent me unto you: this is my name for ever, and this is my memorial unto all generations.*** (KJV) When He said His name would be remembered, He meant it.

Why should we care about any of this? Because we are destroyed for lack of knowledge. When we see the word LORD in all capital letters in an English Bible we should be reasonably confident it is where the name יהוה would be found in the original Hebrew. The first time the tetragrammaton is used can be found in Genesis 2:4 ***These are the generations of the heavens and of the earth when they were created, in the day that the LORD God made the earth and the heavens.*** (KJV) The words LORD God would be found in the Hebrew written this way—אלהים יהוה and again not to make light of this title, it would be similar to saying Judge John, identifying the proper name with the proper title. Knowing the difference between a name and a title is important to understanding the way in which Biblical writer is speaking about God to someone else in the bible.

If we use the example, *he washed his car*, who's car was washed? Did he was his own car or was he washing a car for someone else? The title of אלהים is not exclusively used to identify the Creator. In what should be a familiar verse Exodus 20:3 ***Thou shalt have no other gods before me.*** (KJV) Obviously יהוה the LORD is the one who is speaking and He uses the אלהים to identify any other divine or imaginary beings by saying you will have no other אלהים before me, or quite literally in My face. When translating any writing out of the original language, it is very easy to create confusion. There are advertisements that can not be used outside of the original language because to do so would be counterproductive. Jokes outside of the original language suffer the same fate as do figures of speech. Imagine trying to use a literal translation of *that's a cool book!* into Spanish and getting something like *es libra muy frio,* the book is very cold. There are places in the Bible where יהוה is identified as Lord (not all capital letters) because of the use of the Hebrew word אדני pronounced adonai. For instance In Genesis 18:1 when יהוה came to Abraham and then in verse 3 Abraham refers to יהוה as אדני out of respect. One would not be so arrogant as to speak to the Creator of the universe without proper respect. In most English Bible it is translated as *The LORD came to Abraham…* in verse 1 and in verse 3 as *Abraham said my lord…* These are the subtle differences in designations that we must be aware of as we study and examine the Bible.

Addressing the pronunciation for the tetragrammaton will not be addressed here. That will be left up to the Hebrew linguists because that is their area of expertise. While there are many (mostly primary English only speakers) who will attempt to prove their theories of how the name should be pronounced, many of them fail the test of linguistics. Some try to use the Strong's Concordance to prove pronunciation. That is like trying to use an English dictionary to speak martian. The name of יהוה is Hebrew. Any attempt to use any other language to force a pronunciation will contain fatal flaws and the result will be wrong. Thankfully there are Many Hebrew language experts who are willing to give the pronunciation using years of dedicated research along with pages of documentation available for scrutiny. What has been available to every English speaker since the King James was first published is an example found in Isaiah 12:2 ***Behold, God is my salvation; I will trust, and not be afraid: for the Lord Jehovah is my strength and my song; he also is become my salvation.*** Having a copy of the 400th anniversary addition of the King James Bible[2] the name Jehovah is spelled *Iehovah* causing the reader to use a familiar Y sound at the beginning of the name. Speculation would suggest that even in 1611, the translators knew how to pronounce the name יהוה.

Finding the characteristics of our Creator can be exciting, in Genesis 22:14 ***And Abraham called the name of that place Jehovahjireh: as it is said to this day, In the mount of the Lord it shall be seen.*** (KJV) יהוה ירהאה The LORD is my provider. Exodus 17:15 ***And Moses built an altar, and called the name of it Jehovahnissi:*** (KJV) נסי יהוה the LORD is my banner. רעי יהוה from Psalm 23:1 ***The LORD is my shepherd.*** There are many more exam-

---

2   King James version 1611 digital reproduction used courtesy of: The Bible Museum 2000 North Litchfield Road Goodyear Arizona 85395 Published by Zondervan.

ples of this throughout the bible, is it any wonder that His title should be plural while He Himself is singular?

In Exodus 3:13 Moses asked a question, ***And Moses said unto God, Behold, when I come unto the children of Israel, and shall say unto them, The God of your fathers hath sent me unto you; and they shall say to me, What is his name? what shall I say unto them?*** The answer wasn't יהוה but instead he said what English readers know a I AM THAT I AM. Why did the Creator choose to be known as I AM? The name, יהוה had been known since Adam and then through Abraham. Moses wasn't seeking something he already knew, he wanted something that only the Hebrew people would understand. The answer אהיה (I AM) assured they would understand this to mean that the one who sent Moses was, is and will always be. There is no beginning and no end there simply is, to exist. Taking that message back to Egypt, to the people of promise gave Moses the courage he needed. Knowing that in that short phrase, I AM, the one who spoke to him from a burning bush could never fail him. He then in Exodus 3:15 gives the command that His name יהוה would always be remembered.

Who is your אלהים? It really is a fair question, for some He is a healer, for others peace, He refuses to be categorized because He is outside of any category but He is in every category. When a craftsman builds a table, we could say he puts his soul into it. What we really mean of course is that he uses all of his skill to make every cut perfect, every joint flawless and each coat of finish is polished in exhausting detail. When our Creator creates, He speaks, His breath, His very spirit is within everything He creates, including each and every one of us. Is it possible to reduce יהוה אלהים to anything less than who and what He is? Of course not, although some have tried—without success.

When Jeremiah cries out ***"Shall a man make gods unto himself, and they are no gods?"*** He realized there would always be people in the world who would be fooled into following man made or worse, self made gods. There would be traditions full of lies that deceive and confuse even some of the most cautious causing them to follow unholy gods. Jeremiah was correct. Throughout history many have chosen to follow gods that are created instead of remaining true to the Creator.

One would like to believe recognizing a charlatan who is trying to deceive would be easy, but we do not live in an ideal world. The unscrupulous people who try to manipulate language and twist scripture have been preying on believers for a very long time. People who have rejected the truth given to us by יהוה on the pages we read in the Bible often view believers as gullible, willing to believe anything that sounds good. Paul writes in 2 Timothy 4:3–4 ***For the time will come when they will not endure sound doctrine; but after their own lusts shall they heap to themselves teachers, having itching ears; And they shall turn away their ears from the truth, and shall be turned unto fables.*** (KJV) One must wonder if Paul is remembering the words written in 2 Chronicles 24:20–21 ***And the Spirit of God came upon Zechariah the son of Jehoiada the priest, which stood above the people, and said unto them, Thus saith God, Why transgress ye the commandments of the Lord, that ye cannot prosper? because ye have forsaken the Lord, he hath also forsaken you. And they conspired against him, and stoned him with stones at the commandment of the king in the court of the house of the Lord.*** (KJV) Realistically, people like to believe what is easy to believe, we're lazy, we enjoy information in small easy to understand morsels that are easy to digest. People have been trained to have someone else do the diligent study and explain what they learned in simple language. When a doctor uses a phrase such as myocardial infarction, many would simply give a blank stare until he puts it in the simpler term, heart attack.

Unfortunately scoundrels make their way through life using this system to get rich ad to promote their own personal agendas. The warning in Jude 1:3–4 ***Beloved, when I gave all diligence to write unto you of the common salvation, it was needful for me to write unto you, and exhort you that ye should earnestly contend for the faith which was once delivered unto the saints. For there are certain men crept in unawares, who were before of old ordained to this condemnation, ungodly men, turning the grace of our God into lasciviousness, and denying the only LORD God, and our Lord Jesus Christ.*** (KJV) These are the people who enter our lives through our worship communities, our entertainment, (TV, radio, music etc.) or our families. They are patient and gain our trust, then they begin to influence us to promote their agenda and to steal. Some may have been educated in Bible colleges or seminaries. They sound good and some even believe what they are doing is building the kingdom of heaven because they have been tricked into promoting someone else's scheme. They use just enough scripture to convince you they are Holy but what they are really doing is twisting and perverting scripture to suite themselves. Who is your אלהים? It is the God or gods you trust because of the information you chose to believe.

MONOTHEISTIC HEBREW OR POLYTHEISTIC GREEK?

THE אלהים OF Abraham, Isaac and Jacob is Holy and righteous, His word and His name will last forever. Deuteronomy 6:4 ***Hear, O Israel: The LORD our God is one lord.*** (KJV) In this short declaration Moses proclaims that אלהים יהוה is one, singular. He alone is the אלהים God of אלהים gods and everything else, there can be not other. This is the very foundation that Moses begins with, *In the beginning God.* Any attempt to inject another god into the monotheistic mindset would be deceptive. When יהוה told Moses to tell the people I AM sent me, they would have understood the only אלהים that has always existed had spoken to Moses. The Hebrew people living in Egypt were very well aware of the numerous gods of the Egyptians. Many cultures throughout history were polytheistic but few were monotheistic. When the mixed multitude left Egypt, they were faced with many obstacles. Overcoming polytheism may have been the most difficult one they faced.

In Exodus 20:3 יהוה shouted out loud and clear His first instruction, you will put no other gods in my face! He demands that everyone and everything respect His supreme authority and this includes the other divine beings as well. As this lesson progresses we learn that eventually Moses returns to the top of the mountain and the people get worried. They were so convinced that their Creator and Moses had abandoned them that they were able to convince Aaron to make an idol but why did they not trust only יהוה at this time? We could speculate that in Exodus 7:1 יהוה said to Moses, **And the Lord said unto Moses, See, I have made thee a god to Pharaoh: and Aaron thy brother shall be thy prophet.** (KJV) The mixed multitude that came out of Egypt had also witnessed the miracles that Moses and Aaron did, it is possible that they thought Moses wasn't simply allowing the spirit of יהוה to work through him but they had accepted Moses as a god also? Remember that these same people begged Moses not to allow יהוה to speak to them any more. Exodus 20:19 **And they said unto Moses, Speak thou with us, and we will hear: but let not God speak with us, lest we die.** (KJV) Basically saying *we will do what you say Moses, but please don't let יהוה speak to us again.*

When Aaron capitulated and made the golden calf, they placed it on an alter and said this from Exodus 32:4–5 **And he received them at their hand, and fashioned it with a graving tool, after he had made it a molten calf: and they said, These be thy gods, O Israel, which brought thee up out of the land of Egypt. And when Aaron saw it, he built an altar before it; and Aaron made proclamation, and said, To morrow is a feast to the Lord.** (KJV) Archeological evidence found at mount Sinai (the mountain of Moses) in the land of Midian reveals they had chiseled images of the gods of Egypt on the alter. Aaron declared these are your אלהים (gods) everyone, tomorrow we throw a party for יהוה. If Moses had not intervened, Israel would have been destroyed. This single event and the following punishments forever changed the mindset for the majority of Abrahams dependents. Most would no longer accept following more than one אלהים and that one would be יהוה.

This staunch monotheistic mindset separated the Hebrew people from the most of the other nations around them. This is exactly what יהוה expects from us today as well. To be separated, set apart and called out is to be Holy. Then and now we are surrounded by a polytheistic world. Of course it is easy to use the Greeks and Romans as an example of this. Luke records this incident in Acts 17:22–23 ***Then Paul stood in the midst of Mars' hill, and said, Ye men of Athens, I perceive that in all things ye are too superstitious. For as I passed by, and beheld your devotions, I found an altar with this inscription, To The Unknown God. Whom therefore ye ignorantly worship, him declare I unto you.*** (KJV) The word superstitious used in the King James actually is religious in the Greek text. Paul was observing their prayers to various gods, just as Jeremiah prophesied so many years ago. the people in that temple didn't understand the concept of worshipping the Creator and not the created. Pauls use of an alter to this unknown god to teach that they didn't need any other god or idols was nothing less than brilliant. Paul's zealously monotheistic mindset was able to shift the thinking of some who heard his words. Others may have not believed what he told them but all Paul needed to do was deliver the message.

The polytheistic belief that there could be any created being that is equal to our Creator is to discredit the sacred word of יהוה. Even today believers argue about the timing of creation compared to the evolutionary theory. Some have a difficult time actually believing the Bible so they try to force the time theory of an evolutionary scale into the scripture by using a couple of verses out of context. Psalm 90:4 *For a thousand years in thy sight are but as yesterday when it is past, and as a watch in the night.* (KJV) And 2 Peter 3:8 *But, beloved, be not ignorant of this one thing, that one day is with the Lord as a thousand years, and a thousand years as one day.* (KJV) Neither of these verses describe time here on earth, they describe that in the presence of יהוה with His untimeliness (because He is forever in both directions) time with Him just doesn't mean much. To touch on a subject some may be thinking here, not every divine being is capable of transitioning through time. If that were possible wouldn't one of the demons or devils have done that by now in an attempt to change the course of humanity? Gabriel tells Daniel he was stopped for 21 days by the divine being who had authority over the geographic location of Persia and needed Michael to intervene for him. Why was he not able to time travel back to deliver the message? Enough of that distraction, Hopefully one can now recognize the importance of using proper names and titles when we are studying the Bible and making certain to include all of the clues, the information that is relevant to the lesson we need to learn from scripture.

The polytheistic thinker readily accepts multiple gods. How unfortunate for Christians that most of their teaching has been from a polytheistic point of view. From the earliest non-Hebrew converts and even the early church fathers to Constantine and Eusebius the polytheistic attitudes were abundant. The rejection of the monotheistic Jewish mindset crippled the consistency of Biblical authority by injecting polytheistic concepts. Prayers to Mary for example would never be considered by a monotheistic person nor would these of idols such as a crucifix. Even the Christian cross has been turned into something to be worshipped as many houses of worship have them displayed in a prominent location with songs chanted to it like prayers to a non-existent god.

The influence of polytheism has far reaching effect on believers. Some even hold onto their idols as they leave this life hoping that a piece of wood or brass shaped like a cross will be carried into heaven with them. We often hear how faithful someone is but when we examine their life we wonder what they were faithful to. Does keeping religious symbols of every shape and size declare your faith in יהוה or does it reveal their desire to include all of the empty traditions they may have learned about? Idols come in all shapes and sizes, Some are larger than life while others are as small as a mustard seed that is placed in a piece of jewelry. Even the tiny mustard seed has become an idol for some simply because of it's size used to describe an amount of faith in יהוה needed to move a mountain. Matthew 17:20 ***And Jesus said unto them, Because of your unbelief: for verily I say unto you, If ye have faith as a grain of mustard seed, ye shall say unto this mountain, Remove hence to yonder place; and it shall remove; and nothing shall be impossible unto you.*** (KJV) As he reminds his disciples their trust must be placed with יהוה if they wish to accomplish anything. Christians today wonder why they can not perform miracles, the answer is found in Exodus 4:21 ***And the Lord said unto Moses, When thou goest to return into Egypt, see that thou do all those wonders before Pharaoh, which I have put in thine hand: but I will harden his heart, that he shall not let the people go.*** (KJV) יהוה tells Moses that the wonders or miracles יהוה puts in his hand. In other words those miracles don't come from Moses, they come from יהוה as conformation directly from the throne room that Moses had the authority to use them. When we don't place all of our trust in יהוה we do not have any authority to expect a miracle. The disciples that are being chastised by Jesus in the Matthew passage are no different than we are today. They were surrounded by the same polytheism that remains in the time we live in now. Their doubt defeated them and it defeats us as well.

The trinity is a cornerstone of many (but not all) Christian denominations, yet there is no mention of it in the Bible. Why? Is it possible that the foundation of many denominations of the three in one is wrong? How can three be one when the Bible, the sacred word of יהוה reads that He is one? Christian theologians will argue that it is described wherever we read about the Father, son and Holy ghost but is that consistent with the rest of the Bible? We know that in the beginning is אלהים יהוה leaving the son for later, examine the Holy ghost or Holy Spirit.

First we need to know what the _Biblical definition_ of spirit is. The widely accepted definition is wind or breath and can be found in any concordance or Bible encyclopedia. Next we need to know if breath can exist before it is exhaled or if wind can move without being disturbed. Wind by definition is moving air, so it can't be wind until it moves. Is it possible for breath to be exist before it is exhaled? Remember that inspiration is breathing in, that isn't the question but we need to prepared for the complete analysis. Consider the time before creation of heaven and earth, did יהוה breathe? John 4:24 **God is a Spirit: and they that worship him must worship him in spirit and in truth.** (KJV) If יהוה is spirit, breath or wind, how is it possible for that spirit to exist twice? Once as יהוה and then again as the Holy Spirit? Of course that is a self defeating circular argument and Jesus certainly must have been trying to explain a more complex concept to the woman with whom he was speaking. To put it in context, he first said those who worship יהוה must worship in spirit and in truth. Exhaling their spirit or releasing their spirit to connect with the spirit of יהוה which is also truth. When we speak we release our spirit just as יהוה did at creation. His breath created and continues to work His will in heaven and on earth. Our spirit causes things to happen as well. When we release a spirit or word of love we should expect to see that manifest in some way, even when it's just a smile on the face of another. When we release an unholy spirit we see that manifest as well, sometimes an angry response from someone or worse. Did יהוה breathe before creation? Did He have a need or desire to? The philosophical questions may be endless. The Bible reads that prior to anything else אלהים יהוה is. That indicates that before He choose to speak and release His spirit, His breath, it could not have existed because אלהיום יהוה created everything including His spirit. That very fact undermines the trinitarian theory. Before יהוה spoke there was no spirit, only יהוה.

The modern polytheistic view tries to justify the problem of the spirit being inside of יהוה before he spoke but the Creator created the laws of physics that apply to heaven and earth. That is almost comparing the eggs in a female or the sperm in a male to having children. Just because they were inside, doesn't mean a baby will be born to the outside. יהוה must speak to release His spirit, and that spirit created heaven first and then our physical universe that we can see, feel and live in. Without some form of action the wind doesn't blow, without parents coupling together a child can not be conceived and without יהוה speaking nothing exists except Him.

The polytheistic mind must be able to include a law-less, orderless heavenly realm, one in which several gods must come together to form one (G)od. The Bible on the other hand, the sacred word of יהוה reads differently. In the beginning אלהים יהוה created and brought light and order to a dark formless nothing. Are we then to believe that יהוה who insists on such a light and orderly existence to surround Him would contend with chaos? That is not the character of יהוה described in the Bible. יהוה brings order to disorder, light to darkness, design to wreck-less abandon and purpose to life. We read this throughout the Genesis account of creation. The evolutionists insist on a destructive beginning to our universe and to the average Bible reader a chaotic beginning seems plausible. However the Hebrew word translated as formless can also mean emptiness or empty space. We could translate Genesis 1:2 as, "The earth was nothing, an empty space, it was so dark that the darkness was overwhelming. And the Spirit of אלהים remained above the water. One may wonder if there was nothing more than empty space where the water comes from and that is a legitimate question. As יהוה spoke and His spirit went out swirling into the empti-ness that spirit created first the waters mentioned and then the land to form what we know as our earth.

If you have ever watched an eddy form in a fast mov-ing current of water, what we see on the surface is flat but underneath it is not. The circular motion we can see on the surface indicates a flow of fluid dynamics below. If one were able to see what was happening in and under that eddy we would witness something amazing. Inside the eddy may seem like nothing more than a disorganized and convoluted mass of confusion but it is actually the result of complex forces that form that swirling turbulence we see. The sprit of יהוה is the force that creates what we are able to see in the universe today. That same force that creates the circular form in an eddy, created the spherical shapes we observe in nature. The result of His spirit moving created the gravity that hold our universe together. When we drop a stone into a pond the splash of droplets are not flat or square, they are spherical. The wave ring we watch is circular, all of these things were designed at creation. What we witness in nature today works exactly the same way as His spirit brings form to His new creation.

The extreme polytheistic approach to creation is to have one god make the water and another make land while still another makes the stars and so on. The Bible has a much easier lesson for us, one Creator, יהוה אלהים. An architect who draws the blueprints for a building has a design in their mind and puts it on paper but that architect typically doesn't build the building by themself. For a universe as complex as the one in which we live, more than one designer or builder would cause confusion. Imagine having a team of biologists attempt to design a simple plant like grass with a root system and how it would absorb the nutrients to feed the leaves, not to mention how the proteins and enzymes would carry those nutrients. Think about how that team would agree on the way the carbon dioxide would be used and oxygen released back into the atmosphere. All of this while another team was woking on a single cell organism let alone a fish or mammal. There can only be one אלהים one designer and one Creator.

Some may attempt to justify the polytheistic theory by saying that these gods operated under one, or as one God. To think that אלהים יהוה would need to have help creating anything is to undermine His authority. Polytheism in any construct, dishonors the majesty of our Creator while at the same time abolishing any Biblical authority. Isaiah 45:5–7, ***I am the LORD, and there is none else, there is no God beside me: I girded thee, though thou hast not known me: That they may know from the rising of the sun, and from the west, that there is none beside me. I am the LORD, and there is none else. I form the light, and create darkness: I make peace, and create evil: I the LORD do all these things.*** " (KJV) Would Isaiah have been able to be a legitimate prophet if he would have included any plurality to this statement? No, Isaiah would have been discredited, killed long before he was and we would not have his writing today.

Polytheists are no different than evolutionists when attempting to interpret the Bible. Where some see more than one אלהים יהוה others see millions of years of creation. Martin Luther (1483–1546) is best known for his reformation movement. In his lifetime the theory wasn't evolution as much as single day or instant creation. He writes this, *"When Moses writes that God created heaven and earth and whatever is in them in six days, then let this period continue to have been six days, and do not venture to devise any comment according to which six days were one day. But if you cannot understand how this could have been done in six days, then grant the Holy Spirit the honor of being more learned than you are. For you are to deal with Scripture in such a way that you bear in mind that God Himself says what is written. But since God is speaking, it is not fitting for you wantonly to turn His Word in the direction you wish to go.*"[3] When יהוה tells us through His prophets that He alone Created the heavens

---

[3] What Luther Says. A Practical In-Home Anthology for the Active Christian, compiled by Ewald M. Plass, Concordia, 1959, p. 93.

and the earth why would we as believers try to twist His sacred word for our convenience? What could we possibly hope to achieve?

If one's desire is to worship more than one god or to have idols to hold on to, would it still be possible to consider יהוה as one's God? Exodus 20:3–5, ***Thou shalt have no other gods before me. Thou shalt not make unto thee any graven image, or any likeness of any thing that is in heaven above, or that is in the earth beneath, or that is in the water under the earth. Thou shalt not bow down thyself to them, nor serve them: for I the Lord thy God am a jealous God, visiting the iniquity of the fathers upon the children unto the third and fourth generation of them that hate me;*** (KJV) Moses records these words shouted from the mountain top and they remain the foundational instructions for Christians and the Jewish people today. יהוה Himself acknowledges He is a jealous אלהים and He demands singularity of worship. Regardless of what man may try to achieve, what agenda we may try to promote or how we may try to convince each other that what we think is right, יהוה existed before anything else and has the ability to outlast anything that He alone created. The saying *people plan God laughs*, most likely comes from Psalm 2:4, ***From his throne in heaven the Lord laughs and mocks their feeble plans.*** (GNT) David begins this Psalm with the question, *"Why is everyone angry and make empty plans?"* (my translation) David looks around and sees the people moving away from יהוה and can't understand why. He knows that in the end יהוה will be victorious but his warning falls on deaf ears. The same thing is happening today, people are not willing to live the way that יהוה designed them to live. Instead they want to go their own way and do their own thing. We have believed the lies from our fathers and we pray to gods that are not gods at all. יהוה does not take any pleasure in making fun of us, He simply allows us the freedom to destroy ourselves, to be our own worst enemy. Yet He is always there and always willing to hear our prayer of repentance, and will accept us back when we are ready to follow His instructions.

The polytheistic world view practically destroyed the children of Abraham on more than one occasion, but He reminds us of this in Malachi 3:6, ***For I am the LORD, I change not; therefore ye sons of Jacob are not consumed.*** (KJV) Imagine if יהוה decided to change gravity, would He make it stronger or weaker? Either way we would all be destroyed. Nothing would function as it should, nothing we had ever made could survive and creation itself wold be in disarray. Because He chooses to remain the same forever (yesterday, today and tomorrow) all of creation has the opportunity to be safe until He chooses to remake Heaven and earth. Isaiah 66:22. *For as the new heavens and the new earth, which I will make, shall **remain before me, saith the Lord, so shall your seed and your name remain.*** (KJV) We are the ones who must change, we are the ones who must conform to His monotheistic mindset. Bowing to any other god or holding on to any idol drives a wedge between יהוה and ourselves. When יהוה spoke and created light the sun was not yet created. David writes in Psalm 18:12, ***At the brightness that was before him his thick clouds passed, hail stones and coals of fire.*** (KJV) יהוה Himself is light and when we allow anything to come between us and Him we are in a shadow. A familiar verse from Psalm 23 reads, ***Yea, though I walk through the valley of the shadow of death, I will fear no evil: for thou art with me; thy rod and thy staff they comfort me.*** (KJV) Even when we are in the shadow, with anything between ourself and

יהוה He is with us. Nothing that has ever been created has that power or authority.

No tradition or denominational doctrine can legitimize a polytheistic reference to אלהים יהוה in the Bible although some try. יהוה is one and that concept is repeated often. The warnings against polytheism are evident as spoken by יהוה at mount Sinai. The punishments for polytheism and idolatry are recorded in many places throughout the Scripture. Today the remnants of polytheism and idolatry are evident in some Christian churches and in some of the synagogues of Jewish believers. Songs and prayers to idols or other gods are offered up just as Jeremiah feared. Thankfully, there does remain those who are faithful as there have always been. Revelation 3:4, ***Thou hast a few names even in Sardis which have not defiled their garments; and they shall walk with me in white: for they are worthy*** (KJV) Is not unlike other prophets have said. There were those who remained faithful in the days of Elijah as well, 1 Kings 19:18, ***Yet I have left me seven thousand in Israel, all the knees which have not bowed unto Baal, and every mouth which hath not kissed him.*** (KJV) and yet again we read in Isaiah 1:9, ***Except the Lord of hosts had left unto us a very small remnant, we should have been as Sodom, and we should have been like unto Gomorrah.*** (KJV) Those faithful few have always endured the hardships, mockery and the persecution from the ones who would bow down to the idols and gods of the day. Described as dressed in white for their purity to the monotheistic mindset that יהוה demands Solomon writes in Ecclesiastes 9:8, ***Let thy garments be always white; and let thy head lack no ointment.*** (KJV) If we claim to believe the Bible, if we claim to acknowledge the God of Abraham, Isaac and Jacob as our אלהים we can not continue to perpetuate the lies we have inherited from our fathers or pray to gods that can not answer.

After Peter spoke to the crowd who was gathered at the temple to celebrate Shavuot, the day יהוה shouted the 10 commandments from the top of Mount Sinai, those who were first part of what would become Christianity were all of Hebrew descendants. As this new *Way* of believing spread, it included gentiles who witnessed the incredible miracles and wanted to be included. These new believers did not know the complete history of the Hebrew people or the way the Hebrew culture understood who אלהים יהוה is. Most new *Christians* did not wake up reciting the Shema, (Deuteronomy 6:4–9) and they were not reminded of the monotheistic mantra of יהוה is one several times each day.

For the new gentile Christians this new God was an extension of what they were familiar with. To the polytheistic mind, the idea that two or three gods having the ability to come together to form one larger, stronger god made perfect sense. Naturally this created a conflict among the followers of the Way often causing these believers to splinter into separate groups. This quick evolution from the Jewish righteous man ישוע Yeshua, into a Greek or Gentile god Jesus, remains a source of conflict and trouble in the world today.

Historians and scholars still debate about the exact dates of the events as they happened but the turmoil between Christian and Jew exploded between the first and 4 century eventually ending in a seemingly unreconcilable division. Constantine receives most of the credit for being the central figure who rejects everything pertaining to the Jews but before he was even born there were those who were changing the course of the new religion. The early church fathers, being Gentile themselves readily accepted the belief in Jesus but rejected the history, culture monotheism that was associated with it. Justin Martyr (100–165 AD) writes in his *dialog with Trypho* (a fictional name for Martyr's literary use) that the new church had every right to change the Sabbath from the 7th day to the first day which is the day of the sun. The polytheistic mind is not restricted by the instructions established by יהוה because if there is more than one god we can then choose which one to serve and worship.

John 20:28, ***And Thomas answered and said unto him, My Lord and my God.*** (KJV) This is the only place in the new Testament where any Jewish person considers Jesus as God. Thomas is a lesser known disciple, also called by the name Didymus. He was from the Galilee area but there is little information about him. The question, *why would Thomas identify Jesus as God?* needs to be examined. The Greek linguists argue that it is written improperly but that is of little value as many of the manuscripts we have contain grammatical errors and inconsistencies. A more likely explanation is that Thomas makes this statement as a figure of speech giving ישוע Yeshua, the titles of lord and (g)od. Just as Moses was a god to Pharaoh so ישוע Yeshua becomes a god to Thomas. Exodus 7:1, ***And the Lord said unto Moses, See, I have made thee a god to Pharaoh: and Aaron thy brother shall be thy prophet.*** (KJV) This explanation would be more consistent Biblically because it is the lacking rebuke that ישוע Yeshua speaks when others attempt to raise him to a position of authority. Matthew 19:17, Mark 10:18 and Luke 18:19 all record ישוע Yeshua as rebuking someone for calling him good. In John 5:30 ישוע Yeshua said he can do nothing on his own, everything is from the Father. Yet ישוע Yeshua does not rebuke Thomas and most assuredly everyone in that room would have recognized a polytheistic statement had one been made.

The colloquialisms of the Jewish society were much different than those of the Hellenistic culture. This is yet another hint that the New Testament was originally written in Hebrew, by Hebrews and later translated into Greek. All of the early church fathers who address this agree. Jerome (342–420) acquired a Hebrew copy of the gospel of Matthew used by the Nazarenes and translated it into Latin. He also writes in his letter known as *On Illustrious Men* (chapter 3) that Mark needed to interpret Peter's letters into Greek. With this information available, one can realize the opportunity for confusion exists only a few short centuries form the original events.

Returning to Martyr's *dialog with Trypho*, Martyr drives a wedge between Jew and gentile by insisting the law was abrogated. Martyr writes in chapter XI, *But we do not trust through Moses or through the law; for then we would do the same as yourselves.* In other words, if we were obedient to the law we would be just like you. Which is a ridiculous statement considering Matthew 5:17–19, **Think not that I am come to destroy the law, or the prophets: I am not come to destroy, but to fulfil. For verily I say unto you, Till heaven and earth pass, one jot or one tittle shall in no wise pass from the law, till all be fulfilled. Whosoever therefore shall break one of these least commandments, and shall teach men so, he shall be called the least in the kingdom of heaven: but whosoever shall do and teach them, the same shall be called great in the kingdom of heaven.** (KJV) If Martyr's reasoning for the law, the first five books of the Bible to have been repealed is the Resurrection of ישוע Yeshua, perhaps he would be better served to know what ישוע Yeshua said. The resurrection did not complete everything that had been established by the law and had Martyr grasped that knowledge, he would not have been so arrogant and jump to his mistaken conclusion. But we must realize that Martyr remained a polytheistic gentile and changing the rules the gods established was nothing new to him. After all as long as we follow the instructions from some god they would provide protection for their servants, wouldn't they?

Christians enjoy turning to the early church fathers for their proof that they believed in the trinity but remember that these early church fathers were in fact primarily polytheistic worshippers before hearing about יהוה. The writings of these men while extremely valuable are filled with evidence of polytheism and must be read critically. They, for the most part were also new to the faith and were trying to understand the things they were being taught just as many new Christians are today. The one thing they didn't have to contend with is the centuries of traditions that we have now.

How is the average believer, either Jewish or Christian to justify what they believe today? Obviously it isn't possible for the Monotheistic Jewish follower of יהוה to accept the polytheistic Trinitarian godhead. Nor will the Christian be convinced that their savior is not Jesus Christ. The ability to dig through the language, culture and history is only a beginning, one must carefully study forensically. Aligning the information properly and chasing the ghosts of misinformation down every rabbit hole until no further fatal flaws remain in the equation. Only then can a proper conclusion be reached. Only then is one able to proclaim they have rejected the lies of our fathers and now pray to the only one who is ready and willing to answer our prayers.

WHAT'S IN A NAME?

Words mean things, without definitions communication between human beings would be similar to the animals. When אלהים יהוה breathed the th of life into Adam, He elevated humanity above the animals. יהוה gave to us the ability of careful thought, more than simply reacting to circumstances or environment. Scientists will point to the similarities in DNA between humans and animals or humans and fruit but what they have not yet found a way to measure is the breath of יהוה that is in every human and not in any animal. It was Adam who gave the names to the animals, Genesis 2:20, ***And Adam gave names to all cattle, and to the fowl of the air, and to every beast of the field; but for Adam there was not found an help meet for him.*** (KJV) This translation gives us the impression that the animals we see today are exactly the same as when Adam named them just after creation or that he named them as we name pets today. Of course that is ludicrous, The original Hebrew teaches us a different lesson. *Adam gave names to all of the beasts, the birds of the air and to every living thing on land but for Adam, no opposite helper was found.* (my translation) At creation there were only a pair of each *kind* of animal. Those pairs held the genetic code for the animals we have in the world today. The animal and bird kinds Adam would be familiar with would have included cats, dogs, horses and other livestock, small and large birds and of course the reptile kinds as well. Each kind would have been named and the names would have most likely had a meaning that described the animal.

When we read about the people in the Bible who were born and given a name, every person was named for a reason. Genesis 4:1, ***And Adam knew Eve his wife; and she conceived, and bare Cain, and said, I have gotten a man from the Lord.*** The name Cain in English is קין in Hebrew the phrase I have acquired is in Hebrew one word קניתי pronounced cān-ē-tē. With just this simple example, one can see the relationship between the phrase *I have acquired* and the name Cain. Every ancient Hebrew name and every modern Hebrew name has a meaning. The meaning of the name Isaiah ישעיהו pronounced ūhāy-ahsəy and it means יהוה saves. Jeremiah, ירמיהו pronounced ūhāy-əm-riy could have 2 very similar meanings, either יהוה will raise or appointed by יהוה.

When we read the translations available we should be aware that often the names we read often can be associated with an action also. This isn't always the appropriate approach because sometimes the name is only describing the person. David דוד for instance means beloved and while there are instances where we could use that meaning in place of his name it just wouldn't make sense to always think King Beloved instead of King David. Names in the Bible can remind us of actions and events or they can humble us as well. The name Adam אדם meaning man, is formed from the soil or dirt אדמה pronounced adōmáh reminding us that our physical bodies come from the earth and will return to the earth when we are finished with it. Whether a given name glorifies יהוה keeps us humble, describes who we are or where we came from, every name is important. Modern parents around the world face the challenge to name their children. Will they be named after a relative or will they have a name that reminds the parent of someone or is the chosen name given because of other reasons. Naming a child has never been an easy task. A name is usually something that a person carries with them all of their lives. Certainly some people have nicknames and some even change their name later but a name remains with us forever even if we move to a different part of the world.

There are some people we read about in the Bible who might confuse us concerning their name. Paul is one of the more interesting persons who's name seems to change depending on where he is. Saul or Sha'ul שאול is first introduced at the stoning of Stephen in Acts 7:58 ***And cast him out of the city, and stoned him: and the witnesses laid down their clothes at a young man's feet, whose name was Saul.*** (KJV) The book of acts describes Saul as consenting to Stephen's murder and persecuting those who have accepted this *Way* of believing and yet it is not made clear as to why until later. In Acts 13:9 we learn something interesting, ***Then Saul, (who also is called Paul,) filled with the Holy Ghost, set his eyes on him.*** (KJV) Notice that the text reads Saul was also called Paul, it does not tell us that his name was changed but that he is known by two names.

In Paul's letter to the Romans he indicates he is from the tribe of Benjamin. Romans 11:1, ***I say then, Hath God cast away his people? God forbid. For I also am an Israelite, of the seed of Abraham, of the tribe of Benjamin.*** (KJV) And in Acts 22:28, ***And the chief captain answered,***

With a great sum obtained I this freedom. And Paul said, But I was free born. (KJV) Saul or Paul held dual citizenship, he was born as a Roman citizen while at the same time he is also a child of Abraham. His name didn't change because of his *conversion,* he had always been known to the Jewish people as Saul or Sha'ul and when he was traveling among the Greek/Roman people he would be called Paul or Paulus. We get more inside from Acts 22:3, ***I am verily a man which am a Jew, born in Tarsus, a city in Cilicia, yet brought up in this city at the feet of Gamaliel, and taught according to the perfect manner of the law of the fathers, and was zealous toward God, as ye all are this day.*** (KJV) Being born in Tarsus made him a Roman citizen but being raised as a Jew in Jerusalem and studying to be a Pharisee he would not have used his Roman name while in Jerusalem. The tradition that Saul's name was changed to Paul after his meeting with Jesus on the road to Damascus fails to agree with the Biblical narrative and we should include that tradition with the lies we have inherited.

Simon Peter is another who seems to have two names. To the casual reader it seems Jesus simply renames Simon as Peter with no real explanation. Typically the simplest explanation would be the best choice. There were two disciples named Simon, one is known as Simon the zealot and speculation is he was related in some way to Jesus. The other is Simon, brother of Andrew. When any group has two people with the same name, one usually gets a nickname. Many believe that the reason Peter was the one who received the nickname is because of the speculative notion the other Simon was either a brother or cousin to Jesus. Simon the Zealot is mentioned few times in the New Testament which has caused him to be considered the most obscure of the disciples. Peter on the other hand has his anecdotes (good and bad, wise and foolish) plastered throughout the New Testament.

When the names of these important Biblical characters are changed, we loose their meaning. Translating from one language into another can be complex. Often there is no *word for word* translation that can offer a complete understanding of what was written in the original. When we think about the lessons we have in Isaiah for instance, how much more enhanced would they be to those who don't speak Hebrew if they would know that Isaiah means יהוה saves, so that as we read this book of the Bible we are constantly reminded each time we see Isaiah's name, יהוה saves. Jeremiah's name, appointed by יהוה should remind us each time we see it, we are appointed by יהוה and He has a plan for our life.

These are not secrete codes or intricate conspiracies, the Bible in its original language is so easy to understand someone hearing it for the first time would be able to do their part with ease. Deuteronomy 31:10–11. *And Moses commanded them, saying, At the end of every seven* years, in the solemnity of the year of release, in the feast of ***tabernacles, When all Israel is come to appear before the Lord thy God in the place which he shall choose, thou shalt read this law before all Israel in their hearing.*** (KJV) This means that a 7 year old child, hearing this for the first time would be able to hear what their responsibilities are and do them. Remember that the children were also supposed to be nurtured in the instructions too, so what they heard should have been very familiar to them. In our modern more civilized society, WE no longer hear most Christian or even Jewish leaders saying *here "is what Moses said to do, now go do it."* Instead we hear excuses, reasons we fail at following the instructions we were given from יהוה.

When we fail to recognize the meaning of a name in the Bible we really don't know who the person is and there are some characters who are not named such as Lot's wife but her fate and her example are used later. Luke 9:62, ***And Jesus said unto him, No man, having put his hand to the plough, and looking back, is fit for the kingdom of God.*** (KJV) Careful reading of the men leading Lot and his wife out of Sodom informs us that because they had been delaying their escape the men took them by the hand to drag them out of the city. Even though she is not named, her infamous act of looking back not only cost her life but it serves as our example not to have a desire for our past.

Some Christians would argue the name Jesus is the most important name in the Bible, here is where they will be disappointed. The letter J didn't appear in the English language until sometime around the 16th–17th century. Prior to that the letter I was used and often placed with an E to produce a variation of the Y sound we know today. To complicate this further, the original sound of the letter J was the Y sound as in Hallelujah which is typically translated as praise the LORD or more precisely, praise JAH, the short form of יהוה. In the King James Bible there remains in Psalm 68:4, ***Sing unto God, sing praises to his name: extol him that rideth upon the heavens by his name JAH, and rejoice before him.*** David's use of this shortened form is not uncommon in the Hebrew Bible. There are 50 places in the original Hebrew text of our Old Testament where the name יהוה is shortened to יה (JAH) Again the pronunciation of the name will be left to the Hebrew scholars, this example is used to associate the letter J with the Y sound that is same as the Hebrew letter י (yod) at the beginning of a word or name. Thankfully David was given this to record in Psalm 44:20–21, ***If we have for-***

gotten the name of our God, or stretched out our hands to a strange god; Shall not God search this out? for he knoweth the secrets of the heart. (KJV) Even though we may have been taught wrongly, when we are seeking יהוה He will guide us to Himself.

Originally the name most English speakers know today as Jesus, is the shortened form of the name Joshua. In it's Hebrew יהושע (yə-hō-shu-ah). This name became the (nickname) ישוע (Yeshua) and the accepted meaning is יהוה is our salvation. The Combination of the Hebrew letters that make the name ישוע (Yeshua) give the name meaning. Exodus 14:13, *And Moses said unto the people, Fear ye not, stand still, and see the salvation of the Lord, which he will shew to you to day: for the Egyptians whom ye have seen to day, ye shall see them again no more for ever.* (KJV) The word *salvation* in this verse is in the Hebrew ישועה pronounced the same Yeshua.

Over the centuries the name ישוע (Yeshua) was changed into the Latin IESVS (Yēsūs) and later into English as IESUS (Yə-sus) until we have the familiar name to day of Jesus, which of course early in the English was still pronounced Yesus as the English language evolved. The English name Jesus may not be the most important name in the Christian Bible after all and one could speculate that if he were walking in any crowd and someone called *Jesus!* to him, he may not answer or he may have a confused look on his face. Much like if someone calls you by another name, they may get your attention but you wouldn't know for certain they were addressing you or someone else. Bear in mind, for the millions of Christians who were taught the name Jesus and had no way to understand his original, real name, there is forgiveness. Just as hopefully we would forgive someone for addressing us by a different name, we can be assured that ישוע Yeshua, will have the understanding that we have inherited the lies and the traditions along with the evolution of language and translation problems that are often the source of our confusion.

For those who take the time to explore the meaning of the names we read in the Bible it is more than a source of information, they can be a valued treasure of inspiration as well. Finding out that Abraham is the father of many nations or Ezekiel means יהוה will strengthen, gives us inside into the lives of these people and their relationship to אלהים יהוה. This treasure trove of insight helps us with our faith today, taking us deeper into Biblical study and allowing us to understand all of the things יהוה wants us to know. The names of the places can be equally inspiring as well. In the valley of Elah, David picked up five smooth stones but have you ever asked where those stones originated? Stones are washed smooth by the constant wear of tumbling in the water, having their sharp edges eroded by the sand and gravel in that waters action as they move downstream until they suitable for use in a sling. So where did David's stones come from? Upstream from where this famous incident happened is a place known as Migdal Oz (mĭg- dâl ōz) which means strong tower. Psalm 61:3 ***For thou hast been a shelter for me, and a strong tower from the enemy.*** Proverbs18:10, ***The name of the Lord is a strong tower: the righteous runneth into it, and is safe.*** (KJV) David and his son Solomon knew exactly what the meaning of this is and they most likely considered it quite literal. Knowing what happened, who was involved and where these events took place brings the Bible to life more so than reading a news report today.

What's in a name? Everything, who a person may be, why a place may be important, There are no coincidences in the Bible. Every person, every place and every event is there to teach us who יהוה is and what He expects from us. Often these events are examples of the consequences for our failure to be obedient. The book of Esther is one tremendous lesson of what can happen when we are faithful and do things His way. Ester and Mordecai didn't have an easy life but they prevented a disastrous outcome. When we follow the genealogy of the people involved in this lesson, we learn so much more about how their lives had been intertwined from before they were even born. One does not need to be fluent in Hebrew or Greek to find the meaning behind the names in the Bible. There are several free resources to draw from that are sufficiently capable of supplying accurate information. Find a reliable source of information and discover for yourself how exciting reading the Bible can be. Allow the names to be more than just people or places, remember the meaning of those names as you read and you may be surprised at what you learn.

CHANGING THE QUESTION

Asking a question is submitting a request for information. When we require information we don't have, we ask someone who should be able provide the answer. Sounds easy, doesn't it? If one wanted to know the sum of 2+2 for example and this person thought the answer should be 5, they may ask a thousand others, *does 2+2 = 5?* Hopefully everyone would tell them *no, the correct answer is 4.* For simplicity, pretend that the thousand people just said, "N*o*" without offering the correct answer. Without the correction has the person actually found a legitimate answer to the question? Yes, they have but it does not answer the the real question. Unfortunately too many approach Biblical questions exactly like the person in the example and they receive answers that are equally insufficient. Type *What does the Bible say about_* (fill in the blank) into any search engine and the results are practically limitless. Articles, videos and all forms of media can be streamed into your device. Everything from people who have dedicated years of their life to Biblical research to those who are promoting their own agenda to the charlatans trying to cash in on your curiosity become available for you to choose from. So how does one know which answer is correct? Try changing the question.

Being specific can yield better results, not just in a search engine but when asking knowledgeable people too. One of the common comments from pastors, rabbis, counselors and other professionals is that people ask generic questions. Of course being trained for this they will often respond with what specifically do you want to know? Attempting to get a better understanding for what the person really wants to receive the answer they need. In a conversation with several Christian pastors the subject of most asked questions arose. The three top topics for this group was marriage, divorce and money and all agreed other pastors would acknowledge the same from among their congregations. One problem exists universally, each pastor will answer any question from the interpretation of their denominational doctrine. So when asking a pastor about Biblical principles, one must phrase their question appropriately by first excluding what that denominations platform is on the subject with which one is inquiring. Being specific enough to force someone to answer not from their own perspective but with Biblical authority is one key to receiving an honest answer.

Another method to being specific is to include book, chapter and verse when asking about Biblical topics. During a conversation someone said, *well, it really isn't in the Bible but we believe...* If it's not in the Bible and you are representing the Bible why would you choose to believe something that can not be found there? This inclusive of many denominations and many people. For some unknown reason people enjoy replacing scripture with their own philosophy. Deuteronomy 4:2, *Ye shall not add unto the word which I command you, neither shall ye diminish ought from it, that ye may keep the commandments of the Lord your God which I command you*. (KJV) Deuteronomy 12:32, *What thing soever I command you, observe to do it: thou shalt not add thereto, nor diminish from it.* (KJV) This was also true of the Pharisees as ישוע Yeshua corrected them. Mark 7:6–7 *He answered and said unto them, Well hath Esaias prophesied of you hypocrites, as it is written, This people honoureth me with their lips, but their heart is far from me. 7 Howbeit in vain do they worship me, teaching for doctrines the commandments of men.* (KJV) Even today many Jewish believers will wash their hands using a negel vasser, (a small pitcher typically with two handles and a bowl to catch the water) before eating bread. No mention of this can be found in the books of Moses, (Genesis, Exodus, Leviticus, Numbers and Deuteronomy) and yet some modern Rabbi's would try and convince you that there is scripture reference for it. Without specific passages from the Bible, traditions and denominational doctrine from any religion should be carefully scrutinized to ensure Biblical authority.

If it sounds too good to be true, it's probably a lie. Everyone likes to think that what they believe is correct. Care must be made when asking a question that one doesn't influence the answer with the question. Children become very adept at using this form of communication. No parent wants to say no to their child and children learn how to manipulate this quickly. Politicians also use this technique to sway voters sales people use it to make sales. No matter how much you argue once a sales person gets you to agree that their product is better you will most likely make the purchase. No matter how much sugar that child has already had once you hesitate with your negative answer, they will get the ice cream or candy. Each one of us seeks positive confirmation for our ideas or actions. No one wants to hear contradictory or negative input for something they have carefully planned or completed. So when we ask a question, it should be neutral. Pollsters are also adept at asking questions that lead us to an answer they desire. Advertisers also use this technique in an attempt to have you try the product or service their clients provide.

On the topic of divorce for instance, one may ask, "Why does God forbid remarrying the same person?" Religious counselors should be ready for this question with an appropriate response but some get manipulated into a lengthly debate on the subject. One could argue that marrying the same person very rarely has a successful outcome, but more importantly just as Lot's wife looked back and was turned into a pillar of salt, having a desire to return to the past is impossible. People are capable of change, however the likelihood of two people being able to forgive each other enough to build the strong, united relationship marriage demands without constantly remembering the things done in the past that led to the divorce is highly unlikely. יהוה desires for us to have a long, productive, successful, fruitful and joyous life, we should be able to learn what works for us and what doesn't. Reuniting with someone who caused us to fail often results in repeated failure. Rather than ask why יהוה forbids remarriage to the same person, the question should be, "How is יהוה able to help me find the person who is right for me to marry?" This question provides a more positive and forward moving approach inclusive of the instructions given to us by יהוה.

When considering marriage, couples of every age would be wise to seek the counsel of their religious leader.

The question of, "Why do you want to get married?" May seem obvious but today people choose to get married for many reasons. Young couples typically desire marriage for love, older couples simply may want constant companionship. Some marry for Biblical reasons and others rush into marriage for purely selfish reasons. Proper premarital counseling should reveal any obstacles that may cause problems in the future and asking direct and neutral questions is necessary to bring any negative inclinations into the open for further discussion. Marriage in the modern western viewpoint is far different from the marriage we read about in the Bible. Care must be practiced when comparing a Biblical marriage to the modern marriage we are use to today.

The Biblical foundation for marriage is to form a functional family unit but that is to the only reason for marriage we find in the sacred word of יהוה. Caring for the widows is extremely important in scripture. Deuteronomy 25:5, *If brethren dwell together, and one of them die, and* have no child, the wife of the dead shall not marry without unto a stranger: her husband's brother shall go in unto her, and take her to ***him to wife, and perform the duty of an husband's brother unto her.*** (KJV) In this verse we see that it is the duty of the living brother (also translated as kinsman or countryman) to marry the widow and care for her as he would his primary wife. He would provide her with her own home and treat her as his wife. This arrangement has very little to do with sexual relations other than attempting to provide the widow with hopefully a male child who when he becomes a man will provide for his mother. Sexual relations were not the primary purpose or function of a Biblical marriage but today most western cultures view marriage as little more than God approved sex. Biblical marriage forms the strong family unit necessary for strong communities and strong nations. The parental role in the Biblical marriage is to provide the children with the instructions from יהוה, this includes learning how to love אלהים יהוה with all your heart, all your soul and all of your might and love your neighbor as yourself.

Philosophers like to ask a question similar to; *what's the meaning of life?* What happens when we change that question to a more direct and positive question. *What is the purpose of man?* Solomon answers that question quite adequately in Ecclesiastes 12:13, **Let us hear the conclusion of the whole matter: Fear God, and keep his commandments: for this is the whole duty of man.** (KJV) After Solomon's entire dissertation he writes that everything is for these two reasons, to love and respect אלהים יהצה who created us and to do as He asks us. Philosophy enjoys asking questions that often led to endless circular discussions but seldom offer fundamental answers. (Of course the philosopher would argue that statement) The Bible on the other hand gives us the answer to all of the questions once we learn how to ask them correctly. Just as as good sales person will always find a way to circle back to their product or service, the Bible will always point us in the direction that יהוה desires for us to go. Jeremiah 29:11, **For I know the thoughts that I think toward you, saith the LORD, thoughts of peace, and not of evil, to give you an expected end.** (KJV) אלהים יהוה has a direction He wants us to go in our life that keeps us content and not anxious. His desire for us is to live the way He designed us to live.

When we constantly ask the same questions and consistently receive conflicting answers, it is time to change the question. The question *Who is God?* Really has no simple answer. As mentioned in an earlier chapter יהוה אלהים has many characteristics. One may see Him as Creator, another as Healer and He is very easily both at the same time. The better question would be, *who is* אלהים יהוה *to me?* Each individual believer needs to know יהוה for themselves. What He is to one person today may not be the way they need to know Him tomorrow. While אלהים יהוה is Almighty and majestic, He still chooses to interact with those who diligently seek Him. This same אלהים יהוה who shouted out the 10 Commandments from Mount Sinai is the same אלהים יהוה who spoke to Elijah in a still small voice. 1 Kings 19:12, ***And after the earthquake a fire; but the LORD was not in the fire: and after the fire a still small voice***. (KJV) Sometimes we need to hear the authority and power of יהוה and sometimes we need to hear the love of a heavenly Father. יהוה is this and more.

To know who יהוה is for the individual, one must be willing to ask what David asks in psalm 51:10–12 ***Create in me a clean heart, O God; and renew a right spirit within me Cast me not away from thy presence; and take not thy holy spirit from me. Restore unto me the joy of thy salvation; and uphold me with thy free spirit***. (KJV) As David repents he asks יהוה to reset his life. He asks for a clean heart and a firm spirit but notice in verse 12 his request is for the joy that comes from the salvation יהוה provides and to be upheld by His generous spirit. David as an individual confesses that on his own his life is in turmoil and he needs the direction that only יהוה could provide. That is who יהוה is to David the day he wrote this, and on other days, when his life wasn't such a mess, his psalms of joy are equally heartfelt.

Who יהוה is to you depends on how much He is included in your life. His instructions are clear that he wants to celebrate with you when you are happy and He is willing to comfort you when you are sad. If we ask, *Is He with us in school?* Yes, if you ask Him to be. *Is he with us when we go shopping?* Yes, and His instructions guide our choices for the purchases we make. Don't ask, *Does God care what I wear?* Change the question to be, *Is this choice going to glorify* יהוה*?* That question could be asked for many reasons, prior to accepting a job offer is one example. Keeping יהוה with us by knowing the ideas and direction He desires for us to go may seem cumbersome but it is't. Once one is able to recognize the many blessing He offers us when we live the way He intends for us to live, we discover the peace and calm that David requested.

Are the instructions difficult? After all the Bible seems so specifically ambiguous about how we are to wear some things or eat some things. There are a few verses that might answer this question. 1 John 5:2–3, ***By this we know that we love the children of God, when we love God, and keep his commandments. For this is the love of God, that we keep his commandments: and his commandments are not grievous.*** (KJV) John tells us the instructions are not terrible or difficult. Deuteronomy 30:11–14 ***For this commandment which I command thee this day, it is not hidden from thee, neither is it far off. It is not in heaven, that thou shouldest say, Who shall go up for us to heaven, and bring it unto us, that we may hear it, and do it? Neither is it beyond the sea, that thou shouldest say, Who shall go over the sea for us, and bring it unto us, that we may hear it, and do it? But the word is very nigh unto thee, in thy mouth, and in thy heart, that thou mayest do it.*** (KJV) The instructions are not hidden or out of our reach. יהוה knows us because He designed us, He would not have us do something that is not achievable. We live in the universe יהוה created, much like children live in their parents home and He provide the rules for His created home. Much like a parent sets rules for children to keep them safe and maintain order and discipline, the Biblical instructions do the same for our our lives.

The acronym **B**asic **I**nstructions **B**efore **L**eaving **E**arth implies that the Bible is an instruction manual. The reality is that the Bible is more of an owners manual for our lives. Just as any complicated piece of machinery would have a book to explain how to operate and maintain it, the Bible does that for our life. There are instructions for how much work we are to do, what is the best fuel for our bodies and even instructions for avoiding hazardous situations. Auto mechanics often talk about how people abuse their cars and doctors speak of the many ways people abuse their bodies. Knowing this the question of *Why don't more people read the owner's manual?* Comes to mind When we want to have our vehicles and other expensive equipment operating at their peak performance levels we refer to the manual. When we want the best from our lives we should refer to the Bible and do what the sacred word of יהוה instructs us to do.

YOU CAN'T TEACH WHAT YOU DO NOT KNOW

Deuteronomy 6:4–7, ***Hear, O Israel: The Lord our God is one Lord: And thou shalt love the Lord thy God with all thine heart, and with all thy soul, and with all thy might. And these words, which I command thee this day, shall be in thine heart: And thou shalt teach them diligently unto thy children, and shalt talk of them when thou sittest in thine house, and when thou walkest by the way, and when thou liest down, and when thou risest up.*** (KJV) Parents are instructed to teach their children so they can teach their children and so on. One problem arises when the parent does not know the instructions. How then is the process to continue? Solomon writes in Proverbs 3:11–12, ***My son, despise not the chastening of the Lord; neither be weary of his correction: For whom the Lord loveth he correcteth; even as a father the son in whom he delighteth.*** (KJV) One way or another we will learn the instructions given to us, either by being taught by a parent or other caregiver or directly by יהוה Himself.

Many believe the saying, *children are a blessing* is found in the Bible but you won't find those exact words. Psalm 127:3, **Children are a gift from the LORD. Babies are a reward**. (ICB) The parental responsibility to teach your children the instructions from יהוה would be useless without a child to teach. In 21st century, there are those who seek extreme measures to receive the gift of a child and conversely there are those willing to go to extreme measures to refuse the gift of a child also. Procreating is the first instruction given to Adam and Eve. Genesis 1:28, **And God blessed them, and God said unto them, Be fruitful, and multiply, and replenish the earth, and sub-due it: and have dominion over the fish of the sea, and over the fowl of the air, and over every living thing that moveth upon the earth.** (KJV) Preservation of life is the second command, telling Adam and Eve they need to eat what is healthy for them to nourish their bodies. The first instinct for the newborn baby is to breathe the second is to nurse. New mothers describe this many different ways and the majority agree that nursing a newborn is like nothing else they have ever experience or will ever experience. The seemingly simple act of offering nourishment to a baby has two distinctly separate components. The physical compo-nent can be taught to the new mother. Showing her how to hold the child and encourage the child and even getting the child to suckle. The emotional aspect can not be taught, the connective maternal bond between mother and infant induces irreplaceable psychological benefits for both. Once a new mother holds that tiny extension of both parents she will forever be, mom.

Fathers on the other hand are provided with a differ-ent kind of union. The father doesn't have the opportunity to offer nourishment because his body is not designed to do so. Historically fathers have the role to provide, protect and preside. This paternal role of nurturer may not be as immediate as the maternal but it is equally important. When a father is present to watch his child grow in a happy home filled with love, his feeling of contentment and accomplishment is immense. Our modern world demands that some families adopt non-Biblical parental roles. Almost the only aspect of parenthood left unchanged is that of teacher. Ideally, the child should begin to learn to trust the parents or others who may be placed in the role of caregiver. This first interaction begins with those who hold the child, keeping him or her in a safe secure and gentle embrace offers the child a feeling of safety. This feeling builds trust and has the potential to affect the rest of the child's life.

When a child fails to achieve a sense of security early in life it may be evidenced through interaction with others. A child who feels safe around others is more capable to part of a team as they feel the people around them should be able to trust each other while the child who fails to have that feeling of security may become more independent. Whether it is a sports team, a group at work or even a military unit the person who lacks trust in their counterparts can be a detriment to the cohesion of the group. Learning to overcome the feeling of insecurity may be difficult for the person who did not have that feeling of safety as a child. More importantly, the person who feels they can not depend on others is less likely to fully and completely rely on יהוה as they mature. Instilling that first feeling of trust in a child is extremely important for extending that trust to יהוה. Proverbs 3:5, ***Trust in the Lord with all thine heart; and lean not unto thine own understanding***. (KJV) If a person is not able to completely trust יהוה that person will rely on no one other than self. This does not mean that someone can not learn to trust others or trust יהוה, it sim-ply means they will have an easier time working within a team or bonding with the invisible spirit of יהוה.

Just as a child needs to be taught a feeling of security, someone who may be new to listening for the voice of יהוה needs sound advice as well. They would be wise to sur-round themselves with people who are familiar with what the Bible really reveals and not the traditions and doctrines of man. Nothing can drive a person away from יהוה than when they think they have been lied to. Psalm 119:160, ***Thy word is true from the beginning: and every one of thy righteous judgments endureth for ever.*** (KJV) David's statement that the sacred word of יהוה is truth comes from his own experiences. He had witnessed first hand the treachery of man and had taken part in it himself. Only when David allows himself to rely on יהוה is he success-ful because when he tried to accomplish anything on his own he only made things worse. David's lust for Bathsheba and his conspiracy to cover up his transgressions led to the death of Uriah. (2 Samuel 11)

David's sins were punished by יהוה in exacting mea-sure according to the covenant in Exodus 22:23, ***And if any mischief follow, then thou shalt give life for life***, (KJV) The child he fathered with Bathsheba became sick and died providing the sentence, life for life. Because יהוה is a gracious אלהים David and Bathsheba were given Solomon as an heir to the throne. Many will not recognize why this needed to happen because we have been taught the inherited lies of tradition. David's conspiracy to murder Uriah was punish-able by the death of his son and the eventual destruction of the united kingdom under Solomon. The instructions were given and the punishment was certain, many peo-ple would wonder why God would cause the death of a child. The only one with the authority to punish the King of Israel was יהוה Himself and He did it according to His instructions. David knew and understood exactly what was happening and why. David's repentance is repeated in the Psalms, his lessons are there for us to learn from.

Psalm 78:1–4, *My people, listen to my teaching. Listen to what I say. I will speak using stories. I will tell things that have been secret since long ago. We have heard them and know them. Our fathers told them to us. We will not keep them from our children. We will tell those who come later about the praises of the Lord. We will tell about his power and the miracles he has done*. (ICB) David's desire for us to continue to teach our children more than just a list of rules and regulations is so that our children will develop the trust they need to follow יהוה. David continues Psalm 78 this way through verse 7, *For he established a testimony in Jacob, and appointed a law in Israel, which he commanded our fathers, that they should make them known to their children: That the generation to come might know them, even the children which should be born; who should arise and declare them to their children: That they might set their hope in God, and not forget the works of God, but keep his commandments:* (KJV) Yes we teach the instructions but we also teach the lessons found in the Bible as well for the purpose that our children have the opportunity to trust יהוה and keep his commandments.

David had forgotten the command not to lust after something he should not have taken. Exodus 20:17, *Thou shalt not covet thy neighbour's house, thou shalt not covet thy neighbour's wife, nor his manservant, nor his maidservant, nor his ox, nor his ass, nor any thing that is thy neighbour's.* (KJV) His future writing is filled with warnings that do everything possible not to forget these matters and the history of Israel is filled with accounts of what happens when we do.

How then are we to teach our children if all we have are traditions and doctrines full of the lies we have inherited? We study. We use every resource available to us so that we can learn. Turning to the Psalms again this time in Psalm 27:8, ***My heart said, "Seek His face." Your face, O LORD, I will seek*** (BSB) David remembers a familiar passage from Numbers 6:24–26, ***The Lord bless thee, and keep thee: The Lord make his face shine upon thee, and be gracious unto thee: The Lord lift up his countenance upon thee, and give thee peace***. (KJV) The word for face and presence in Hebrew is almost synonymous. David's use of the word here could very easily be meant he needed to seek out the presence of יהוה but there is a better translation for these verses. May Yehovah bless you and guard you, *May Yehovah lift His eyes toward you and offer you and abundance of grace. May the light of Yehovah's face shine brightly on you and remove all of the chaos that causes you unrest.* Imagine being able to stand in the light that is emitted from the face of יהוה. You could feel His presence and His love. This blessing that Aaron was instructed to speak over the children of Israel was so the name יהוה would be spoken over them with all of the power and authority that would be included. That is where we should find ourselves as we study His sacred word.

A growing number of Christian pastors have confessed (to me and others) that for them being a pastor was nothing more than an easy sales job. They would stand in the pulpit and parrot back the things they learned from seminary. During the week they would comfort those who would mourn or help the needy and do all of the things they were expected to do. A few would be caught in an illicit affair or skimming money and loose their job. But when you surround yourself with people who have a strong faith and continually praise יהוה for their blessings, Sometimes something amazing happens. Either they begin to believe the lies we have inherited and become a spokesperson for their denomination or they begin to believe what they read in the Bible. The latter can be devastating to a church more than the former. Imagine a Christian pastor telling the Sunday school director there will not be a Santa Clause or a snowman included in the nativity play this year. What happens when a Christian pastor begins to actually teach the things from the Bible that are different from the traditions the church is comfortable with? He or she will typically be searching for a new church unless the congregants are willing to repent and seek the face of יהוה. More and more churches are doing exactly that, they are diligently searching for the truth. Often when they find the truth they don't quite know what they should do but they are willing to learn. There are also Jewish synagogues of some denominations that are also abandoning their non- Biblical traditions to better align themselves with the sacred word of יהוה which is a fascinating phenomenon. They often face a more harsh persecution from their Jewish brothers and sisters than the Christians face from theirs. This doesn't mean that the Jewish believers are becoming Christian any more than the Christians are becoming Jewish however, both are attempting to worship יהוה the way He chooses to be worshipped and they are beginning to live the way יהוה designed them to live.

The struggle to eradicate the lies we have inherited breaks the boundaries of religion and denomination. The traditions that drive a wedge between יהוה and humanity do not discriminate. One of the most important aspects we can teach our children is that we don't know or understand everything and that we are trying to learn too. As the children mature, including them in that learning process continues to build the trust in relationship and displays to them that an eagerness to learn should never end. Many churches that have Bible study groups segregate the men from the women and the children from the adults. The belief is that separating by age or sex creates commonality but it happens at the cost of excluding new and original ideas. Allowing younger or even new believers to listen to in- depth discussions may be overwhelming for some and yet be stimulating for others. Separating teenage and young adult male and female hormones may be a good idea for many events however a well led (and well supervised) Bible study can produce well balanced and insightful young people who should be learning what יהוה expects from them.

Of course the trouble with attempting to teach what we do not know is a lack of practical knowledge. Just because one may have watched a video of someone else welding one piece of metal to another does not make the observer a welder and no one who has never held a welding stinger should ever attempt to teach another to use one. Likewise just because you have read Genesis chapter 1 does not offer you the authority to teach creation. There are people who spend years in depth and detail study of Genesis 1:1 alone and are willing to admit they still do not fully comprehend the entirety of it. This isn't meant to be taken as no one has the authority to instruct others concerning the sacred word of יהוה, it simply means that reading a passage in only 1 translation does not properly prepare anyone to teach that passage. Obtaining practical knowledge takes time and commitment. Both the welder needs to understand the way the metal flows when the arc is struck and a musician needs to understand the instrument they play before either can teach.

For the parent who does nothing more than send a child on the Sunday School bus, hoping they will receive some sense of morality or religion fails to appreciate their own dilemma. They have surrendered their responsibility to a third party and some will complain when the child rebels. How often do we hear parents say things like *I don't know what happened I sent you to Sunday School.* The uninvolved parent isn't even trying to teach or to learn. They have capitulated to the evils of the world and the child is able to recognize it and use it against them. They are leaning on their own understanding because they were not properly instructed. Proverbs 22:6, ***Train up a child in the way he should go: and when he is old, he will not depart from it*** (KJV) An hour of Sunday School falls far short of Deuteronomy 6:7, ***And thou shalt teach them diligently unto thy children, and shalt talk of them when thou sittest in thine house, and when thou walkest by the way, and when thou liest down, and when thou risest up.*** (KJV) The Bible contains the instructions needed to raise our children to be successful and productive. Fortunately there are many resources available for parents to learn from. Because we can't teach what we don't know, the parental responsibility is to learn. Including a child as we learn demonstrates the importance we place on the subject we are studying.

As a young mother was sitting in a church service, her baby became *cranky.* Not wanting to disturb the people sitting around her as the child began to cry she stood up to leave. The speaker who was not the regular pastor that day stopper her with this statement, *there's no need to leave, that child is welcome to praise God the only way it know how.* The mother nervously sat down to the dismay of some of the older people in the congregation and the speaker, seeing the looks on their faces, began addressing the importance of including children during worship. *If all we are going to do is send them away, how will they learn?* This question cuts through the immediate situation. How would the mother learn what was being taught that day? How can anyone learn when we remove them from the discussion or the lecture?

There is a story about the obviously less fortunate person who walked into a church only to be asked to leave because his presence offended some of the people. This person didn't say anything to offend anyone, they didn't like the way he dressed and the person was unwashed. What did that person learn? That particular person learned that they were welcome at the local drinking establishment. That person leaned that an unholy spirit was more welcoming than the Holy Spirit was in the church. That person learned that church was not the place for them. This story isn't fiction, it has happened too many times.

There is a small but growing community and a local business owner learned they had a terminal illness. The owner reached out to the church next door and offered to sell them the property at a very reduced rate which the church refused. A short time later another business person purchased the property to turn it into a restaurant. The church began a petition against the restaurant because it would be serving alcohol. When a neighbor asked why the church was so against the restaurant they were told by the pastor, *We don't want those people there, they are drinkers and we don't think its going to be a good place.* The neighbor after some thought asked the pastor a pointed question, *The good LORD went to the trouble to bring sinners within inches of your door and you don't want them there!?* Again this is a true story and the surprising part is that after the restaurant was finished, the drug dealers who used the church as cover had to leave because there was so much more activity around the restaurant.

These true stories are examples that you can't teach what you don't know and what happens when you try to teach what you don't know. Would anyone board an airplane if the pilot had not been trained by another experienced, competent pilot? Probably not, yet there are pastors today who are leading churches who have graduated from Bible colleges and seminaries that have been taught by professors who confess they no longer believe the Bible.

Searching for a place where one is able to surround themselves with people who are familiar with יהוה is easy. Finding a place where the people are diligently digging through the language, culture and history for the truth in order to separate the traditions away from the scripture is difficult. Modern churches advertise musical events, dinners or fundraises to attract people to their message when they should be advertising their message to attract people to their music and dinners so they don't need the fundraisers. Around the world advertising companies have found that adding churches to their client list can be very lucrative. What possible reason would a church need to hire an outside advertising firm? Money would be the number one reason. For a church to receive donations it needs to attract people to donate. Someone who is seeking a place to meet people who are more than simply familiar with God, may want to avoid the advertising megachurch. There are a growing number of smaller fellowships that are more capable of meeting your needs. Most of these groups are local and meet in each others homes with little fanfare. Their main purpose is to get to know יהוה and understand His instructions. Most are welcoming and willing to answer questions. Discretion and caution is always a good idea when meeting new people, make sure that you have not accidentally stumbled into someplace unsafe, there are unscrupulous people in the world who want nothing more than what you have.

Some churches have smaller groups in them that bond together to create a wonderful atmosphere where one has the ability to learn without the distractions of tradition or denominational doctrine. These *subgroups* invite speakers who would not normally be allowed by the pastor to speak to the whole church, especially when the church doctrine is in conflict with the Bible. Often they are able to have specialty classes to introduce Hebrew and Greek language basics and some have invited Rabies to teach. Locating a group such as that may be as easy as riding past a church sign or checking the calendar on their website. Of course a call to the pastor or church office can be productive too but that often comes with the obligatory invitation to *come check us out.*

Attempting to learn in order to teach may have some negative side affects but it certainly has no drawbacks. The side affects may include frustration or disheartenment but even learning where you don't want to be is productive. There have been many, many people over the course of the centuries who have listened to only a few teachers or pastors or even Rabies and never questioned a single word they heard. They honestly believed that because these learned people had achieved the position they had that they automatically knew more than anyone else. What these inexperienced people may not have known was if these learned men had learned only the lies they inherited from their fathers. Did they ever stop to question what they were taught? Can they prove using only the Bible what they are saying is, in fact, true?

Few schools of higher education remain that actually teach their student how to read the Bible critically. Most Bible colleges and seminaries are content to teach tradition and denominational doctrine in place of scripture. Humanity owes our gratitude to the few schools who are willing to instruct students how to view the Bible as a whole document and encourage original thought. These are the students who dig through countless ancient manuscripts to find for themselves the exact places where they encounter differences. One such place is in John 6:4, ***And the passover, a feast of the Jews, was nigh***. (KJV) This verse is not be found in the older manuscripts and the confusion has added at least an extra year to the timeline for the ministry of ישוע Yeshua.

With the majority of schools allowing the perpetuation of the lies we have inherited the serious Bible student is often persecuted for questioning the validity of the interpretation. Original thought is denounced as heresy and the discouraged student either gives up and follows the mainstream or is forced to leave what is familiar to follow the narrow path. Being called to go where one is sent by יהוה is nothing new. Abraham, Moses, and many others were instructed to leave a place of comfort and go accomplish what they were asked to do. One famous messenger, Jonah, finally went after a great deal of inconvenience and the message he delivered saved a nation.

There is a growing number of people who study the Bible extensively and exhaustingly without ever setting foot in a formal classroom of higher education. One tremendous benefit for these people is that they are never subjected to the restrictive views of a human professor. They are free to read the Bible and think for themselves without the filters installed by traditional education. These men and women acquire libraries filled with different Biblical translations, commentaries, language study guides and other resource material. They spend countless hours researching for the entire ancient use of a single word or phrase. They understand the difference between a figure of speech and a metaphor used in the Bible. These are the people who read PHD papers and books written by long forgotten writers to find if their revelation can be confirmed or if it was nothing more than speculation.

Gabriel was speaking to Daniel when he foretold that this would happen. Daniel 12:4, ***But thou, O Daniel, shut up the words, and seal the book, even to the time of the end: many shall run to and fro, and knowledge shall be increased.*** (KJV) We are living in a time when the average person who is seeking to be in the presence of יהוה is receiving informative revelation. They are going from place to place to see for themselves the archeology and the writings of that are part of Biblical history. The ancient languages are coming alive once again to share their secrets. Knowledge is increasing, and it is not always increasing among the scholars who are self segregated in their traditional and doctrinal arenas but among the people. Slowly the lies we have inherited are being eroded away to reveal the truth that is the sacred word of יהוה.

Noah, Abraham or Moses had no degree of higher education. We should not degrade the work of the people today who earn any degree. What we should question is the criteria by which the work is judged. The disciples of ישוע Yeshua were simple men and many were fishermen. The prophets were primarily farmers or shepherds although Jeremiah and Ezekiel were priests. All of these people had something very important in common, each one was willing to hear יהוה, to listen and then act on what they were told to do. No one needs a degree of any kind to teach what is revealed in the Bible. What is necessary to teach is a desire to be in the presence of יהוה and a willingness to follow His instructions. The person who would follow the traditions and doctrines of men and reject the instruction of יהוה is in no position to teach others about יהוה because they can not teach what they refuse to learn.

THINKING OUTSIDE THE BOOK

Extra-Biblical writings contain a great amount of information and although some were included as part of the Bible most were never included for various reasons. The books of the Apocrypha was written about 400 years before before ישוע Yeshua and was accepted by Jewish believers as true but not necessarily sacred. It was included in Bibles printed in English until 1881 when two men, Brooke Westcott and Fenton Hort who were textual critics of the time spoke against the Apocrypha as heretical. The Apocrypha was removed form Protestant and Anglican Bibles but remains part of the Catholic Bible. The disagreement concerning the Apocrypha is an example of how people are fallible. One person reads something and has the inclination that it may be true or at the very east valuable while another reads the same thing and considers it heresy.

The book of Enoch is another extra-Biblical writing that has faced much scrutiny with good reason. While it is mentioned in the Jude 1:14–15, ***And Enoch also, the seventh from Adam, prophesied of these, saying, Behold, the***

Lord cometh with ten thousands of his saints, To execute judgment upon all, and to convince all that are ungodly among them of all their ungodly deeds which they have ungodly committed, and of all their hard speeches which ungodly sinners have spoken against him. (KJV) This book of Enoch was not completely written by Enoch. To confuse matters more, the book we have today's not the same writing that would have been known and accepted in the 1st century when the disciples were writing their letters.

The Jewish people of the second temple period would have been familiar withe the stories in Enoch but the later book is not found in any classic Jewish text. the Modern version we have today contains descriptions of the separation between Jew and gentile, a separation that comes from post Grecian invasion rather than from the Old Testament. Exodus 12:48–49, *And when a stranger shall sojourn with thee, and* will keep the passover to the Lord, let all his males be circumcised, and then let him come near and keep it; and he shall be as one that is born in the land: for no uncircumcised person shall eat thereof. One law shall be to him that is homeborn, and unto the stranger that sojourneth among you. (KJV) Moses writes that those who are not natural born children of Abraham are welcome to join themselves to the Israelite people if they are willing to follow the instructions from יהוה. we see this also repeated in Ruth 1:16, ***And Ruth said, Intreat me not to leave thee, or to return from following after thee: for whither thou goest, I will go; and where thou lodgest, I will lodge: thy people shall be my people, and thy God my God:*** (KJV) Ruth being a Moabite made chose to become part of the Family of Abraham. The linage for a Jewish person comes from the mother and so David being a descendant of Ruth would not have been qualified to be king if Ruth would have been considered a Moabite. This inclusiveness is lost in the modern book of Enoch. Also absent is any agreement for the dat of which it is actually written. Linguists and other scholars use various methods to date writings such as the way letters are formed, words used and even figures of speech familiar to other known writings. With Enoch, the date of writing is between the 1st and 4th century BC. As the writing is copied the more opportunity to add or change the document exists. Even though one can easily discern the value in Enoch, it must be read carefully and critically and should never be considered the sacred word of יהוה.

Would the writers of what we consider the New Testament consider the letters they wrote to be equal to scripture? Probably not, yet today while most Christians consider these writings sacred as written, discriminating readers would only consider sacred what those writers actually penned as sacred. All of the additions, corrections and other modifications should not be considered sacred. How do we know the difference? A general rule of thumb would be, *if it can not be verified in the Old Testament it should not be considered sacred*!

As stated in an earlier chapter the early church fathers were primarily polytheistic, their commentaries concerning the New Testament writing have become commonplace Christian theology. The destruction of the second Temple in Jerusalem left the Hebrew followers of ישוע Yeshua vulnerable to persecution. What ישוע Yeshua had taught them was to ignore the rules of the Pharisees and do follow the instructions from יהוה that Moses had written. The polytheists had a different view of ישוע Yeshua, for them ישוע Yeshua was their god and equal to יהוה.

The post crucifixion extra-Biblical writings, seem to possess a surreal feeling of manipulated polytheism. The Pseudepigrapha, is a collection of writings dating from approximately 300 BC to 300 AD. Often included are items such as letters of Pilate and Herod. Many of these works can not be verified and most need to be treated as counterfeit. The common thread that binds these writings with the exception of the Jewish writings, is that ישוע Yeshua has taken the place of יהוה. The Jewish writing included in the Pseudepigrapha have a distinctly hellenistic style of writing on their own. The influence from the Greek and Roman invasion is unmistakable and it worked both ways. The Jewish influence on the Greek invaders was so strong that the Greek magicians began using the name of יהוה in their incantations. The Pharisees who learned of this were as eager to hide the name as their Greek counterparts. The name of יהוה is so powerful that even the Greeks who used it were witnessing miracles. In order for the Greek gods to be upheld they forbade the Jews to speak the name. Many priests refused to be silenced and were killed for continuing to speak the name of יהוה. In the 2nd century Haninah ben Teradion, refused to stop saying the name and was wrapped in a wet Torah scroll and burned at the stake. When he was asked why he refused to obey the Roman order, he answered, *I do as יהוה commands me.*

The infamous *chain letter* from *Jesus* is an example of counterfeit writing. In this letter Jesus supposedly writes to have your work finished by 6:00 on Saturday to be prepared for the sabbath. The trouble with this should have been obvious but many fell for the hoax. The only one who has the authority to change anything that יהוה has established is יהוה Himself and He does not change. Just as ישוע Yeshua tells us in Matthew 24:36, ***But of that day and*** *hour knoweth no man, no, not the angels of heaven, but my Father only.* (KJV) If ישוע Yeshua didn't know when יהוה would cause this world to pass away he certainly does not have the authority to change the Sabbath.

The letters and commentaries of the early church fathers as mentioned previously contain polytheistic concepts, but to disregard them completely would be to ignore the insight they contribute. Not only do we learn more about the disciples but we catch glimpses of what they thought of each other too. Tertullian (203–250 AD) writes a dissertation known as *Against Praxeas*, Praxeas who lived at the same time is an obvious polytheist who believed that the trinity existed before יהוה. Tertullian's arguments are not completely monotheistic however he does at least separate the Father from the son when he writes, *He says that the Father Himself came down into the Virgin, was Himself born of her, Himself suffered, indeed was Himself Jesus Christ.*[4]

Tertullian's view differed in that he believed the son was divine and part of the Father but not equal to the Father. When reading these early Christian writings, one often gets the impression that our modern arguments often revolve around the same discussions. Practically two centuries have passed and the argument remains because the cognitive function of mankind has contrived a misguided attempt to replace יהוה with ישוע Yeshua. The Jewish majority of the 1st century rejected the message of ישוע Yeshua to obey יהוה because they believed ישוע Yeshua wanted people to follow him. Later the Greek followers of ישוע Yeshua persecuted the Jewish believers because they were holding onto the idea that יהוה was one and ישוע Yeshua was only

---

[4]   Against Praxeas, Translated by Dr. Holmes. Electronic version copyright © 1996 by New Advent, Inc.

His prophet. The Greek believers wanted a man-god to worship. What we are left with is a hybrid religious system that has mutated into a convoluted debacle.

Generally, the early history of written language included only actual events or communicating what was absolutely necessary. Writing took time and the mediums of writing were difficult to produce and expensive. Fictional stories were spoken until the advent of easier to produce writing paraphernalia became more commonplace. Though writing is a tremendously efficient way to communicate it is not without complication. The problems that remain were and most likely always will be, the evolution of language and the translation from one language into another. Attempting to transmit a complex idea from one person to another is difficult enough when both are standing next to each other speaking the same language but when someone reads another's writing, clarity is crucial.

The example used earlier, *he washed his car*, leaves much room for confusion. The first people who translated the Bible into English made use of the pronouns and other generic words for many reasons, one is when translating from Hebrew the way some words are conjugated they point to the subject being referred to and it made perfect sense to the translator. Another reason was to save precious paper, shortened words meant less paper (or other medium) needed to write the translation on. Often names were shortened for the same reason. To transliterate (ישעיהו (ūhāy-ahsəy Isaiah, into English the name is easier to change rather than attempt to extrapolate all of the pronunciation each time. When translating through several language changes the problem escalates.

Westcott and Hort ran into this situation when they translated the New Testament. They firmly believed that the only manuscripts worthy of translating were the Vaticanus and the Sinaticus. The Vaticanus was kept in in the Vatican while the Sinaticus was located from St Catherines Monastery. They further believed the Textus Receptus manuscript used to translate the King James to be inferior, Hort writing that the Texts Receptus was *villainous and vile*. Textus Receptus simply means received text and includes many of the Greek manuscripts of the New Testament. Bibles translated from the Textus Receptus include the 1611 King James, Tyndale, Geneva, And Young's Literal Translation. Other Bibles such as the American Standard Version and the New World Translation use the Westcott and Hort translation of the New Testament.

The Old Testament of the Bible is not without controversy, while there is no question the original was written in Hebrew, there are slight variation of the remaining Hebrew manuscripts as well. Legend likes to imply that the ancient scribes meticulously copied every letter perfectly, making certain not to include any mistakes. These scribes were only human and there are some variations between the texts used to translate the Old Testament. There are three main texts used, the Masoretic text, the Westminster Leningrad Codex and the Alepo Codex. The few variations between these writings is mainly technical and can be the result of writing patterns changing over the years. With no vowels in the original Hebrew until the adoption of vowel points used in the Masoretic text, other Hebrew letters were used to indicate the sounds we consider vowels.

Of the Hebrew works, the Alepo Codex is the crown jewel. today it resides in the Shrine Of The Book Museum in a neighborhood of Jerusalem. The Museum also houses the Dead Sea Scrolls and the roof is designed to represent the top of a clay jar similar to what the scrolls would have been found in. Copied in the 10th century by Shlomo Ben-Buya'a, from a scroll that was (allegedly) from the Temple courtyard in Jerusalem, the Alepo Codex appears perfect. Often described as *if an angel wrote it,* the Alepo Codex is considered by the majority of scholars as the authoritative text for the Hebrew Bible, the Christian Old Testament.

Knowing this information may cause one to ask which Bible to choose? The generic answer is the one you will read, but there is more to the answer. For general reading, a translation that is comfortable is recommended. The depth of study will decide which study Bible(s) one would choose. For study one should avoid the paraphrase editions, these Bible are not translated directly from the Hebrew or greek but are simply, slightly varied wording from a translation. There are a few passages in the paraphrase Bibles that are more accurate than the original they are taken from. However these tiny points of light, no matter how bright they shine are obtained at the expense of sifting through endless pages of editorial agenda and scattered errors in the rendering.

Returning to the New Testament, there are recently discovered manuscripts from Spain and India, written in Hebrew and verified to be from sources of the 1st century. These exciting discoveries reinforce the early Christian writings that indicate the Gospel letters were all written in Hebrew. They also offer credit to Paul who is a self described zealot would have continued the tradition of writing about spiritual matters only in Hebrew. Although they have not been completely translated as of the date of this writing, one of the previews does seem to clarify the occupation of ישוע Yeshua as a young man.

These new discoveries together with known Hebrew writings of the New Testament such as Matthew's gospel copied by Shem Tov in the 14th century from an earlier version are shining light on the way the people understood them at the time they were written. Matthew 23:1–3, ***Then spake Jesus to the multitude, and to his disciples, Saying The scribes and the Pharisees sit in Moses' seat: All therefore whatsoever they bid you observe, that observe and do; but do not ye after their works: for they say, and do not.*** (KJV) Careful reading from the different manuscripts offer a slightly different variation that clarifies this passage with the discrepancy being in one word found in verse 3. Instead of whatsoever *they* bid you, we read *he* referring to Moses. Verse 3 makes perfect sense when translated as; **All therefore whatsoever {he} (Moses) bid you observe, that observe and do; but do not ye after their works: for they say, and do not.** This verse now indicates that the Pharisees do not follow what Moses writes instead of trying to twist it into, the Pharisees don't follow what they had written themselves. All of this while addressing the crowd that was gathered instructing them not to follow after their works, the rules they have added because they say one thing and do something else.

This was the last public humiliation the Pharisees could bear, having ישוע Yeshua blatantly tell the crowd to disregard the rules of the Pharisees and then to chastise and degrade them. This was the final straw that would cause the Pharisees to find a way to destroy ישוע Yeshua, but more about that in another chapter.

As Gabriel's prophetic words to Daniel are brought to fruition we witness knowledge increasing and information able to be communicated faster and easier than ever before. We travel physically, visiting the places we have the availability to access. The places that are too far or too expensive we visit virtually. Having access to books and articles from around the world at our fingertips. Technology gives us the opportunity to see places in real time or in three dimensional format. Are we now able to read the things that Daniel was told to seal in a book until the time of the end? The best answer to that questions may be *we will know it when we see it.* The better question would be, *Will this affect our faith in any way?* Yes it will. For some this new information will strengthen their trust in יהוה, for others their faith may not be shaken but the way they apply their faith to their lives may need to change.

How many new discoveries will be revealed to us? We have no way of knowing. Our trust and our worship needs to be completely centered on יהוה, now is not the time for a crises of faith. Now is the time for repentance and prayer. Wild speculation during these current perilous times is useless. Careful analyzation of the information is crucial for maintaining Biblical authority. We should never be too quick to Jump to conclusions as we work through these things in fear and trembling before יהוה.

The sacred word of יהוה as it was originally given through Moses and the prophets is perfect. Even the letters in the New Testament penned by those who were willing to allow יהוה to use their hands for HIs purpose were perfect. Today we have awkward additions that create confusion and sloppy subtractions to imply contradiction in the Bible. Additionally there are those who would re-write the-Bible to promote their own worldly agenda. The extra-Biblical writings deemed unworthy by some as scripture remain invaluable as a witness to the time in which they were written. The copied manuscripts of scripture material recently uncovered bring some clarity back to what had been corrupted. Together these writings help us identify the real words of יהוה from the words of mortal man.

LET THE HERESY TRIAL BEGIN

THE BACKGROUND TO this point is necessary to prepare the reader for the examination of exactly who ישוע Yeshua is and what purpose he fulfilled during his life. The reason for using the Hebrew names אלהים יהוה and ישוע serves these purposes. To reduce the confusion between the titles of LORD and lord, to offer the proper respect to both and to separate the two so that יהוה remains one.

The Christian trinitarian will be offended and needs to be offended. As alluded to in an earlier chapter, there is no triune god, that is a polytheistic fantasy that can not be proven Biblically because it conflicts with Exodus 20:2–3, ***I am the LORD thy God, which have brought thee out of the land of Egypt, out of the house of bondage. Thou shalt have no other gods before me.*** (KJV) Clearly as יהוה is formally introducing Himself to the mixed multitude, He specifically uses His name and His title to ensure everyone knows there is only one of Him. the statement, *Thou shalt have no other gods before me,* literally, you will not put any other gods in my face, should be sufficient in any language.

The polytheistic trinitarian concept is from Matthew 28:19, **Go ye therefore, and teach all nations, baptizing them in the name of the Father, and of the Son, and of the Holy Ghost**: (KJV) There are several problems with attempting to turn this verse into a trinitarian doctrine beginning with the way it is written. There are other places in the New Testament where ישוע refers to himself as the son of man and even a son of יהוה but never as only *the son*. Even Eusebius in his *Ecclesiastical History*, Book III. 5.ii: writes, *But the rest of the apostles, who had been incessantly plotted against with a view to their destruction, and had been driven out of the land of Judea, went unto all nations to preach the Gospel, relying upon the power of Christ, who had said to them, "Go ye and make disciples of all the nations in my name."*

Textual variants and extra-Biblical writings aside, what did the disciples of ישוע actually do? The book of Acts addresses this as there is no account of anyone being baptized in the trinitarian way. There are 4 accounts of people being baptized in the name of either Jesus (ישוע) or the *lord*.

- Acts 2:38, **Then Peter said unto them, Repent, and be baptized every one of you in the name of Jesus Christ for the remission of sins, and ye shall receive the gift of the Holy Ghost.** (KJV)
- Acts 8:16, **For as yet he was fallen upon none of them: only they were baptized in the name of the Lord Jesus.** (KJV)
- Acts 10:48, **And he commanded them to be baptized in the name of the Lord. Then prayed they him to tarry certain days.** (KJV)
- Acts 19:5, **When they heard this, they were baptized in the name of the Lord Jesus** (KJV)

What the Christian church considers baptism was nothing new to the 1st century Jewish community. The practice of cleansing one for repentance had been done since the time of the Tabernacle in the wilderness. Exodus 30:20, ***When they go into the tabernacle of the congregation, they shall wash with water, that they die not; or when they come near to the altar to minister, to burn offering made by fire unto the Lord:*** (KJV)

Water is the first compound building block created (Genesis 1:2) and is so important that only one letter is added to the Hebrew word for water (מים) to become heaven (שמים). Water is used as a physical representation of the spiritual realm. 1 Samuel 7:6, ***And they gathered together to Mizpeh, and drew water, and poured it out before the Lord, and fasted on that day, and said there, We have sinned against the Lord. And Samuel judged the children of Israel in Mizpeh.*** (KJV) In this passage water is used as a physical representation of the sins of the people being poured out or confessed to יהוה.

When one washed or immersed in water for repentance or purification, it was done with moving water. The movement of the water offers the physical feeling of sins being carried away. One would be able to see the water moving, hear it, feel it, taste it and depending on the source, smell it. Every sense given by יהוה was used to sense forgiveness that was sought, and the sinner would take a breath and completely submerge, opening the eyes and mouth to rinse away what we have seen and said. Upon emerging the exhaling breath would cary with it any *unholy* spirits that were residing in the body and that next breath would be taken remembering that it is the breath of יהוה His spirit that was present as He spoke creation into existence.

Why would the disciples baptize in the name of ישוע only and not in the name of יהוה? To answer that question one need to remember that every name has a meaning. The meaning of ישוע is יהוה is our salvation. As the disciples instructed the people to wash or immerse themselves (no one was held onto and *dunked*) They would be reminded that יהוה will rescue them and that is precisely consistent with what every generation had heard since crossing the Red Sea. Exodus 14:13, ***And Moses said unto the people, Fear ye not, stand still, and see the salvation of the LORD, which He will shew to you to day: for the Egyptians whom ye have seen to day, ye shall see them again no more for ever.*** (KJV) The word salvation in this verse is conjugated ישועת (yeshu-aht) because the next word describes who is doing the action of saving, יהוה. The *He* of course refers back to יהוה as well. Since this epic and historic event the Hebrew people understood that any rescue comes directly from יהוה and He will use whoever He chooses to deliver that salvation.

Exodus 2:10, ***And the child grew, and she brought him unto Pharaoh's daughter, and he became her son. And she called his name Moses: and she said, Because I drew him out of the water.*** (KJV) The definition to draw out, is slightly vague in this verse. It can also be used as deliver, there is a song that is sung today, כאלהינו אין *Ain Kaylowhaynoo* the first line is, *there is none like our God, there is none like our LORD, there is none like our king, there is none like our deliverer.* The Hebrew word used here for deliverer is כמושיענו k-mō-she-ā-nū. Even an untrained ear can hear the Hebrew name Moshe in the word which is the name English readers know as Moses. This song celebrates יהוה as our אלהים our king and our deliverer, just as Moses was the one who would physically show the way or deliver the mixed multitude to Mount Sinai, other people throughout history have lead the children of Abraham in various ways. The judges guided Israel after the death of Joshua, then the kings ruled over Israel until the division of the kingdoms of Israel and Judah. After the exile there was a time of turmoil including a corrupted priesthood and finally the Greek and Roman occupation ruled over the land and the people until the destruction of the Temple. Finally after nearly two thousand years, Israel became a political nation once more. This time with a more modern approach toward government with a President and a Prime Minister.

Through all of history no form of a government lead by men who believed that יהוה would stand with them ever succeeded. Only when the men sought to align themselves and the nation with יהוה was Israel successful. by the same token, individuals are only truly successful when they align themselves with יהוה and live the way they are designed to live.

The modern Christian baptism ritual certainly does not resemble the repentance or purification immersion known to the levite priests at Mount Sinai or the early church. Today different denominations have different rituals and depending on the denomination one can expect to be either dunked or sprinkled. Most Christians have never heard of the מקוה mĭk-veh', a word commonly used to describe a baptism among Messianic and Hebrew Roots believers. This term however is not exactly precise, a מקוה mikveh is only a collection of something (usually water) and describes the area in which the immersion would take place.

When ישוע healed the blind man on the Sabbath, he gave him this command found in John 9:7, ***And said unto him, Go, wash in the pool of Siloam, (which is by interpretation, Sent.) He went his way therefore, and washed, and came seeing.*** (KJV) The pool of Siloam was a מקוה

mikveh, a pool used for immersion. What ישוע was telling the man was not to go wash the mud from his eyes, ישוע told him to go and רחץ rachats, bathe in the מקוה mikveh to purify himself as he would know how to do.

The descriptions of what ישוע and the disciples actually did in the New Testament concerning what we know as baptism do not follow the widely accepted account of Matthew 28:19. They acts of ישוע and the disciples follow the instructions given through Moses for repentance and purification. Astute Bible readers will remember John 4:2, (***Though Jesus himself baptized not, but his disciples,***) (KJV) The use of parentheses in the King James Bible are used for two purposes, one is to indicate a thought within a thought and the other reason is to indicate a phrase that was not included in the original manuscripts. While technically correct ישוע did not hold anyone under water for a baptism, what we read in John 9:7 indicated he did indeed send others to רחץ rachats, bathe for purpose of repentance.

The language of Matthew 28:19, fail to read as if someone actually spoke that way combined with a completely different narrative for what the disciples actually did and the realization that spirit/breath can not exist prior to being released is probably not enough to convince the confirmed trinitarian that the polytheistic triune god is a fantasy. The doctrine and traditions of men that have evolved over the past 2,000 years are interlaced with the lies and prayers to gods that don't exist are exactly what Jeremiah warned us about.

Acts 2:1, ***And when the day of Pentecost was fully come, they were all with one accord in one place.*** (KJV) To know where this event occurred, one needs to realize there were more than just the twelve core disciples present along with the women who were following also. The small upper room where the disciples slept would not be large enough to accommodate all of the persons who were present. Not to mention the account which follows states a *multitude* came together because of what they had heard and may have seen also. Luke indicates later in verse 46 that while the disciples were in Jerusalem they were constantly at the temple. ***And they, continuing daily with one accord in the temple, and breaking bread from house to house, did eat their meat with gladness and singleness of heart,*** (KJV). We are given a specific place in the Temple where ישוע and his disciples would gather. John 10:23, ***And Jesus walked in the temple in Solomon's porch.*** (KJV) And again in Acts 5:12, ***And by the hands of the apostles were many signs and wonders wrought among the people; and they were all with one accord in Solomon's porch.*** (KJV) Solomons porch is an area on the east side of the Temple grounds where even the women were allowed. This area would easily accommodate all of the disciples and the women and would also be an area where the people who would be in the vicinity of the Temple could hear with no trouble at all any disturbance that would draw attention, such as the sound of a mighty rushing wind.

Imagine being in Jerusalem for the feast of Shavuot celebrating the day the ten commandments were shouted down from the top of Mount Sinai and having the ceremony disrupted. Being curious, the people began investigating the disturbance possibly expecting some Roman interference, when what they witnessed was completely unexpected. Shavuot is one of the three appointed times that every Hebrew man is instructed to be in Jerusalem, the other two are Passover and Sukkoth (Feast of tabernacles) Which is the reason that the list of places given in verses 9 and 10 are included.

What these people heard was each person not only speaking in the usual languages spoken in Israel at that time, Hebrew and Aramaic but they heard these people speaking in their native language. Deuteronomy 5:22, ***These words the Lord spake unto all your assembly in the mount out of the midst of the fire, of the cloud, and of the thick darkness, with a great voice: and he added no more. And he wrote them in two tables of stone, and delivered them unto me.*** (KJV) this is one of the verses used to describe that each person at Mount Sinai heard the voice of יהוה speaking directly to them. Remember, it was a mixed multitude that came out of Egypt, not everyone spoke the same language. So majestic was the voice of יהיה that not only did the people hear the voice, they actually were able to *see* His voice. Exodus 20:18, ***And all the people saw the thunderings, and the lightnings, and the noise of the trumpet, and the mountain smoking: and when the people saw it, they removed, and stood afar off.*** (KJV) The English is not well translated because it probably didn't make sense to the translator that one would be able to see the voice so it was translated as *thunderings*. What the people witnessed was the power and authority and weight contained in the voice of יהוה. There simply are no English words to convey the awesomeness of such an event. Even if one were deaf they would be able to see, feel and distinguish the words of יהוה on that day. He truly is able to communicate with everyone who will hear or see His voice.

In Jerusalem about 1,300 years after יהוה spoke at mount Sinai He used all of the disciples present to speak so that everyone would hear clearly in their own language. Remember this was not just the twelve first disciples who were speaking, there were most likely over 100 disciples on Solomon's porch that day. Acts 1:15 records about 120 but that is in parentheses. A frequent question asked is, *was this speaking in tongues?* There are other explanations for this that are more plausible. Although the main languages were Hebrew and Aramaic, the location of Israel brings travelers from all over the known world and there very well may have been disciples from all of these regions. There is a saying that the simplest explanation is probably the most accurate could be applied to the disciples this day. They were so overwhelmed by the Holy Spirit that they simply began speaking in their most familiar language. The people hearing this would be confused because they may have believed that all of the disciples would be from the same place as יֵשׁוּעַ and mistakenly assumed they were all Galilean.

The Christian tradition that the Holy Spirit is responsible for causing the disciples to speak in a language unknown to them begins to decay when one considers the more fascinating miracles happening on that day. For instance, only יהוה would be able to gather together that mixture of people from the regions mentioned to proclaim His glory, that is a miracle. Mimicking the sights and sounds first seen and heard at Mount Sinai (although with less fanfare) to capture the attention of the celebrating crowd. That is a miracle. Causing so many that day to reject the traditions and doctrines of men, repent and return to His instructions, that may be the most impressive miracle of the day.

Peter's first response to the accusations of drunkenness is fairly weak. Acts 2:15, ***For these are not drunken, as ye suppose, seeing it is but the third hour of the day.*** (KJV) Shavuot is a celebration, a time to relax and rejoice. The practice of imbibing was readily accepted. Because this is a pilgrimage feast, the instructions from Moses were sometimes taken literally. Deuteronomy 14:24–26, ***And if*** *the way be too long for thee, so that thou art not able to carry it; or if the place be too far from thee, which the LORD thy God shall choose to set his name there, when the LORD thy God hath blessed thee: Then shalt thou turn it into money, and bind up the money in thine hand, and shalt go unto the place which the LORD thy God shall choose: And thou shalt bestow that money for whatsoever thy soul lusteth after, for oxen, or for sheep, or for wine, or for strong drink, or for whatsoever thy soul desireth: and thou shalt eat there before the LORD thy God, and thou shalt rejoice, thou, and thine house-hold.* (KJV) Not to advocate anything, these appointed times are for rest and relaxation as much as they are for worship but worship is the main purpose! Peter's objection to the time implies that if it were later in the day those who were mocking the disciples for being drunk may have been legitimate. Yet again, when someone is under the influence of alcohol they tend to return to their native language.

Peter knows his audience, he knows that if anything that comes from his mouth in any way can be considered blasphemous he and all of the other disciples would be killed immediately. Peter doesn't rely on his own knowl-edge, he turns to the prophet Joel to begin his oration. The quote from Joel chapter 2 holds a key to understanding that Peter is not attempting to replace יהוה but uphold His glory and honor. The quote in Acts 2:21, *And it shall come to pass, that whosoever shall call on the name of the LORD shall be saved.* (KJV) is not complete. Read Joel 2:32 with the name replacing the title, *And it shall come to pass, that whosoever shall call on the name of יהוה shall be delivered: for in mount Zion and in Jerusalem shall be deliverance, as יהוה hath said, and in the remnant whom יהוה shall call.* (KJV, modified)

Peter goes on to speak of ישוע as a *man* which יהוה approved, confirming his actions by allowing the miracles to be accomplished. In other words, the miracles ישוע was able to perform were because יהוה gave them to him. Don't think that ישוע was the only righteous man in Israel at the time or that others were not performing miracles as well. Luke 1:5–6, ***There was in the days of Herod, the king of Judaea, a certain priest named Zacharias, of the course of Abia: and his wife was of the daughters of Aaron, and her name was Elisabeth. And they were both righteous before God, walking in all the commandments and ordinances of the LORD blameless.*** (KJV) Also Simeon was devout in Luke 2:26. There are extra-Biblical writings of others also, Honi the circle maker is a great example of someone who was able to perform miracles. When it didn't rain Honi, drew a circle in the dust and said to יהוה *I won't move until it rains.* When it began to sprinkle he asked for more and it began to pour rain, he ask for a calm rain and the rain calmed. His tomb can be visited today in Hatzor HaGlilit in the Galilee.

As Peter continues his dissertation, he recounts the events of the past few weeks asserting that everyone there knew what had happened. They knew about the crucifixion and the resurrection and Peter proclaims David a prophet for writing about these events. Then Peter gets to a point where many of us today get confused, he is recorded as saying in Acts 2:36, ***Therefore let all the house of Israel know assuredly, that God hath made the same Jesus, whom ye have crucified, both lord and Christ.*** (KJV) There are some textual variants in this verse but that is not where the confusion is. The use of the word lord in this verse is what causes the confusion. Peter does NOT equate ישוע to יהוה the Greek is clear this is not θεός Theos, God, but it reads κύριος, kurios, lord. A more simple way to understand this is Peter is saying that ישוע is elevated above the people standing there much like a king is elevated above them. (More on this later)

The interesting part of the narrative is found in verse 40, ***And with many other words did he testify and exhort, saying, Save yourselves from this untoward generation.*** (KJV) The other words are not recorded and with good reason. Had these words been allowed to be recorded every follower of ישוע would use them and expect every one who heard those words to become a follower too. The message Peter delivered to the people present that day was for their enlightenment, no future generation has experienced the events which those in the early 1st century experienced. Many people have tried to recreate a similar circumstance but have failed because they relied only on their own understanding or have attempted to deliver a false impression of Jesus in place of the ישוע that Peter had first hand knowledge of.

None of the gospel writers ever introduced ישוע as יהוה, they always separated the two. 1 Peter 1:3, ***Blessed be the God and Father of our lord Jesus Christ, which according to his abundant mercy hath begotten us again unto a lively hope by the resurrection of Jesus Christ from the dead,*** (KJV) Notice the way Peter separates אלהים יהוה from ישוע. This separation occurs in the gospel of Mark and in all of the epistles that begin a greeting in the same manner. The book of Hebrews eludes to it this way in Hebrew 1:1–2, ***God, who at sundry times and in divers manners spake in time past unto the fathers by the prophets, Hath in these last days spoken unto us by his Son, whom he hath appointed heir of all things, by whom also he made the worlds;*** (KJV) Thus the writer of Hebrews does not equate ישוע to יהוה, but to the prophets as to consider ישוע a prophet of יהוה.

The separation between יהוה and the person ישוע is necessary to build hope in the resurrection of the dead. There were at least three distinct factions in the political and religious arena of 1st century Israel. The Pharisees, the Sadducees and the Essenes. Of these the Sadducees did not recognize the resurrection of the dead as sound doctrine. The Sadducees rejection of the resurrection forced a divide between the growing number of disciples of ישוע and the rest of the Jewish population. The view that יהוה would not allow the resurrection of the dead and it instead was either blasphemous or demonic is what allowed the persecution of the early followers of ישוע. The Sadducees didn't claim that the resurrection of ישוע didn't happen, they simply declared it was not something יהוה would permit.

To this end the disciples preached the resurrection that much more, using the writings of the prophets to justify that it was indeed יהוה that sanctified the resurrection to give mankind the hope that after the new heaven and new earth was in place, those who were faithful to the covenant between mankind and יהוה would have a place there. Naturally this concept did not conform to the rules of the priests who enjoyed their own power over the people. Having a movement that suggested the rules made by man held no authority over the Torah, the first five books of the Old Testament, was counter-productive to the authority of the high priest. Offering the general population the hope of eternal life on the new earth with the only legal mandate being do what יהוה tells us to do disintegrates the obligation to the man made rules imposed by the pharisaical council and to many modern Christian doctrines. This new *Way* of believing was really nothing new but a return to living the way יהוה designed us to live.

A prime example of this can be found in Acts 18:5–6, ***And when Silas and Timotheus were come from Macedonia, Paul was pressed in the spirit, and testified to the Jews that Jesus was Christ. And when they opposed themselves, and blasphemed, he shook his raiment, and said unto them, Your blood be upon your own heads; I am clean; from henceforth I will go unto the Gentiles.*** (KJV) Had Paul simply preached that the person ישוע was the messiah, he would have been laughed at and scorned. The idea that a dead man could be a king would have been considered ridiculous. But, Paul preaching that the dead ישוע had been resurrected in a permanent sense would put him in direct conflict with the Sadducees in the synagogue. The hostilities between Paul and the Sadducees who refused to believe in the resurrection of the dead is the cause for Paul to go next door and teach the gentiles.

The polytheistic view that *Jesus is God* should not be considered legitimate for one very important reason. Had ישוע been a god or a divine being on earth prior to the resurrection there would be no hope for the resurrection of the dead because he would have been a resurrected divine being. Only by ישוע being completely human would mankind have any hope in the resurrection of the dead. Only being completely human would the blood of ישוע have the authority to pay the price of redemption for mankind.

A JOB DESCRIPTION FOR THE PROPHET

DEUTERONOMY 18:15, ***The LORD thy God will raise up unto thee a Prophet from the midst of thee, of thy brethren, like unto me; unto him ye shall hearken;*** (KJV) The promise of a prophet greater than Moses himself was offered to the people, not just any prophet but *THE PROPHET!* Some have considered Elijah to have been the prophet that Moses spoke of however there is the verse in 1 Kings 19:16, ***You are to anoint Jehu son of Nimshi as king over Israel and Elisha son of Shaphat from Abel-meholah as prophet in your place.*** (HCSB) Because Elijah was told to anoint another prophet to take his place he could NOT be The prophet promised. Malachi 4:5–6, ***Behold, I will send you Elijah the prophet before the coming of the great and dreadful day of the LORD: And he shall turn the heart of the fathers to the children, and the heart of the children to their fathers, lest I come and smite the earth with a curse.*** (KJV) Elijah is promised to return with his own purpose which is not in the job description of *THE PROPHET.*

The forensic evidence in the Bible is the testimony of the Biblical writers. The search for clues is not always found in the surrounding verses but are more often than not recorded by a different hand. As Moses continues his discourse in Deuteronomy 18 he writes in verse 18, ***I will raise them up a Prophet from among their brethren, like unto thee, and will put my words in his mouth; and he shall speak unto them all that I shall command him.*** (KJV) The words of ישוע as recorded in John 12:49, ***For I have not spoken of myself; but the Father which sent me, he gave me a commandment, what I should say, and what I should speak.*** (KJV) There are other places where John records similar statements ישוע makes that are considered by most Christians are more messianic than prophetic. If ישוע can only say and do what he has seen the Father יהוה do one should be able to look into the Old Testament and find where it is written and compare the words and events.

John the Baptist denies being *THE PROPHET* but testifies he is only a voice preparing the people to get ready. The one who is coming, John acknowledges he is not worthy to untie his sandals implying that he would make himself known in John's lifetime. The strange *confession* recorded in John 1:20, ***And he confessed, and denied not; but confessed, I am not the Christ.*** (KJV) comes after the the priests and Levites ask him *Who are you?* In verse 19 needs to be broken down and explained. Practically everyone who reads the Bible should remember that the priests were all supposed to be from the tribe of Levi. The interruption of this lineage came as a result of the Babylonian exile and the Greek occupation in the land of Israel. 2 Maccabees 4:7, ***But Seleucus died, and when Antiochus surnamed Epiphanes succeeded him on the throne, Onias' brother Jason obtained the high priesthood by corrupt means:***

(KJV Apocrypha) The corrupt means used was the ability of Jason to purchase the office of High Priest. Jason was not a Levite nor were many others who held the position of high priest until the fall of the second temple in either 68 or 70 AD depending on whose calendar one chooses to believe accurate. These priests and Levites who asked John the Baptist *Who are you(?)* most likely would be from the council of the Sanhedrin, a group acting with the authority of a *Supreme court* in an occupied country.

The translator's use of the word confession in this verse is not without critique. John didn't admit to anything, he does acknowledge the question from the group and he does proclaim he is not the Christ. The Greek word translated as confession ὁμολογέω (homologeó) can also be translates as being in agreement or making a public declaration. Many people viewed John the Baptist as an outcast, however he did develop a great number of disciples. One could speculate that John's unorthodox lifestyle may be a result of his childhood. Being about six months older than his cousin ישוע he would have been included in the children under two years old that Herod wanted to have killed. That account in Matthew 2:16, ***Then Herod, when he saw that he was mocked of the wise men, was exceeding wroth, and sent forth, and slew all the children that were in Bethlehem, and in all the coasts thereof, from two years old and under, according to the time which he had diligently inquired of the wise men.*** (KJV) His mother Elisabeth could easily have retreated with the child to a place farther into the hill country escaping the orders of Herod. John denying that he is not the Christ or *THE PROPHET* was not without his own problems that shortly would lead to his beheading.

What we discover in the gospel accounts is that John the Baptist was asked if he was *THE PROPHET* but not one ever asks that question of ישוע. The closest one could imagine to ישוע being asked this question is found in Matthew 11:2–3, ***Now when John had heard in the prison the works of Christ, he sent two of his disciples, And said unto him, Art thou he that should come, or do we look for another?*** (KJV) A similar account of this event is found in Luke 7. The transcriptions of this conversation in Matthew and Luke do not offer any conclusive evidence to the average reader, however the answer ישוע offers could allude to them being told to decide for themselves who he is. Luke 7:21, ***Then Jesus answering said unto them, Go your way, and tell John what things ye have seen and heard; how that the blind see, the lame walk, the lepers are cleansed, the deaf hear, the dead are raised, to the poor the gospel is preached.*** (KJV) These are not the actions of a political leader, these are the actions of a prophet.

In order to clarify the difference between prophet and messiah, one needs to understand exactly what a messiah is. To the Christian today a messiah is someone who has been appointed and anointed by God to save sinners from hell. That definition is far from the political or even religious definition of the Hebrew culture at the time ישוע lived and before. Not until later, sometime around the 14th to the 15th century did the word messiah become synonymous with the term savior.

The first time we see the Hebrew root word משח (mahshakh) from which the word משיח (messiah) originates is in Genesis 31:13, ***I am the God of Bethel, where thou anointedst the pillar, and where thou vowedst a vow unto me: now arise, get thee out from this land, and return unto the land of thy kindred.*** (KJV) referring back to when Jacob had his ladder dream in Genesis 28:18, ***And Jacob rose up early in the morning, and took the stone*** *that he had put for his pillows, and set it up for a pillar, and poured oil upon the top of it.* (KJV) Of great importance to note here is that the act of anointing does not make one a king or savior, it is however, a way to physically designate a special person or place. Anointing a rock or a pile of rocks with oil is a way for us to physically express, see and do something that reflects a spiritual bond that we can not see.

The first mention of משיח (messiah) is found in Leviticus 4:3, *If the priest that is anointed do sin according to the sin of the people; then let him bring for his sin, which he hath sinned, a young bullock without blemish unto the Lord for a sin offering.* (KJV) In this verse we recognize a priest is anointed, משיח (messiah) and it is also associated with the consequences of sin.

At the risk of over simplification, the act of anointing is משח (mahshakh) and the one anointed is then משיח (messiah). With this older definition in mind there have been many messiahs throughout Hebrew history. The priests in the wilderness were anointed by Moses and Aaron, Samuel anointed King Saul and King David, even Elijah anointed Elisha. The Greek word Χριστός (Christos) was the nearest word in the language to describe anointment. Etymology (word origin) of the Greek Χριστός we learn is derived from χρίω (chrio) meaning to rub, smear or anoint. Perhaps we should be thankful that the ones translating the gospels into Greek didn't choose the word καταχέω (katacheó) meaning to pour, as their source to describe the Hebrew משיח (messiah) or today we could have a completley different name for Christian.

As one should be able to discern the evolution of the language along with certain traditions has conditioned generations to adopt doctrines that are inconsistent with what the writers of the Bible intended. The lies we have inherited from our fathers and their fathers before them have escalated to such a degree that one must search diligently to find the truth that was being communicated through those writers long ago.

The question ישוע asks Peter, (Matthew 16, Mark 8, Luke 9) *Who do you say that I am?* Along with Peter's answer, *You are the* משיח (*messiah, Christ*) now should require us to ask, What exactly was Peter's idea of what a משיח (messiah) was at the time. Had Peter been thinking ישוע would be a political leader? That was soon put to rest in the response ישוע made to Peter's statement. Mark 8:31, **And he began to teach them, that the Son of man must suffer many things, and be rejected of the elders, and of the chief priests, and scribes, and be killed, and after three days rise again.** (KJV) This can not be considered the way any political leader would speak. No one in history has ever began a political career telling his supporters that they would be killed. This is however the speech of someone who was very familiar with the fate of prophets of Israel.

Luke's record of what was said may shine more light on Peter's answer. Luke 9:20, **He said unto them, But whom say ye that I am? Peter answering said, The Christ of God.** (KJV) Better translated, *You have been anointed by* אלהים יהוה, brings insight and consistency into the conversation. With this answer the political aspect is removed and the religious characteristic is focused on יהוה.

The faction of political leaders in Israel at the time were walking on the same tightrope as the leaders in every other occupied country, attempting to be viewed by the citizens as being in charge while appeasing their Roman rulers. Any political dissension brought by a different contingent had the opportunity to create more tension that would result in a more suppressive rule. ישוע and his disciples were seen as upsetting the status quo which is the same thing that caused John the Baptist to be killed. John's public reprimand concerning Herod divorcing his wife to marry his niece was stirring up trouble. As the disciples of ישוע began to grow in number the Pharisees considered this a political movement causing them to fear for their power and safety. Attempting to label ישוע as a political figure would make quieting him and his disciples easier than allowing him to become a religious leader. The larger problem the Pharisees faced was that by the time they realized ישוע was not interested in playing politics there were already many miracles attributed to him making him more famous as a righteous man.

Luke 23:3, ***And Pilate asked him, saying, Art thou the King of the Jews? And he answered him and said, Thou sayest it***. (KJV) Also in Matthew 27:11 and Mark 15:2. The short answer by ישוע could be translated as *Hey, you said that, not me*. The accusation brought to Pilate forced the political aspect of the situation. Pilate didn't need any political trouble but his actions prove that he didn't believe this to be a political problem. Pilate was an unwilling participant in the crucifixion, the only way to stop a rebellion being encouraged by some of the Pharisees was to capitulate and give the order that ישוע be crucified.

Isaiah is considered to have written much of the messianic prophecies but practically no one mentions his writings concerning *THE PROPHET*. Critical reading and forensic comparison are needed to discover what centuries of inherited lies and tradition has corrupted. Beginning with Isaiah 42:1, ***Behold my servant, whom I uphold; mine elect, in whom my soul delighteth; I have put my*** *spirit upon him: he shall bring forth judgment to the Gentiles*. (KJV) Is there someplace in the Bible where this takes place? Yes, there is, Matthew 3:16–17, *And Jesus, when he was baptized, went up straightway out of the water: and, lo, the heavens were opened unto him, and he saw the Spirit of God descending like a dove, and lighting upon him: And lo a voice from heaven, saying, This is my beloved Son, in whom I am well pleased.* (KJV) What should stand out here is not that יהוה sends His spirit like a dove or that He speaks so that others were able to hear it., what should be a red flag in this verse is that יהוה uses the word servant. Would יהוה consider Himself or part of Himself a servant? Could one even consider that as part of His majestic character?

Isaiah 42:2, *He shall not cry, nor lift up, nor cause his voice to be heard in the street.* (KJV) The humility of the servant is evident in this verse, compare this to Philippians 2:7, *But made himself of no reputation, and took upon him the form of a servant, and was made in the likeness of men*: (KJV) The description of this servant is becoming amazingly similar. Isaiah 43:7, *To open the blind eyes, to bring out the prisoners from the prison, and them that sit in darkness out of the prison house.* (KJV) And in John 9:7, *And said unto him, Go, wash in the pool of Siloam, He went his way therefore, and washed, and came seeing.* (KJV) Some would argue that the tradition of using the title משיח messiah to refer to ישוע is respectful. What we are beginning to discover is that title is not accurate in the original language. Linguistic evolution has created a hybrid definition. The signs and wonders (or miracles) that are described as being performed by Moses, Elijah or even ישוע all originate from יהוה exactly as he told Moses they did. Exodus 4:21, *And the LORD said unto Moses,*

When thou goest to return into Egypt, <u>see that thou do all those wonders before Pharaoh, which I have put in thine hand</u>: but I will harden his heart, that he shall not let the people go. (KJV) Every miracle comes directly from יהוה, we are nothing more than a conduit for His power and authority.

Isaiah 42:8, ***I am the*** [יהוה] ***LORD: that is my name: and my glory will I not give to another, neither my praise to graven images***. (KJV) John 14:28, ***Ye have heard how I said unto you, I go away, and come again unto you. If ye loved me, ye would rejoice, because I said, I go unto the Father: for my Father is greater than I***. (KJV) ישוע is careful not to elevate himself in any way. He often rebukes others for attempting to make him more than he is. Luke 18; 19, ***And Jesus said unto him, Why callest thou me good? none is good, save one, that is, God***. (KJV) When ישוע was asked what is the greatest commandment his first response was to quote Deuteronomy 6:5, ***And thou shalt love the Lord thy God with all thine heart, and with all thy soul, and with all thy might***. (KJV) This verse was and is usually the second verse every Hebrew child has learned since Moses wrote the words *Hear O Israel* יהוה *your* אלהים *is one,* יהוה *is one.*

As the Prophet that Moses prophesied would come ישוע appears to meet all of the criteria using the information we have available today. He is born of his countrymen, he is able to do even greater things than Moses did and he had conformation from heaven to do these things. In the famous words of many sales giants—*But wait, there's more!*

Isaiah 54:16, ***Behold, I have created the smith that bloweth the coals in the fire, and that bringeth forth an instrument for his work; and I have created the waster to destroy***. (KJV) Before the use of the word created is discussed, one would be best suited to conclude who is being spoken of in this verse. While some translations use the more restrictive blacksmith that would be out of context. A חרש (charash̓) is more than just someone who is accomplished in only one trade. Also defined as craftsman, jeweler, mason and yes, carpenter. Interestingly the Hebrew New Testament manuscripts mentioned earlier also use either the same word or similar word in Matthew 13:55, *Is not this the carpenter's son? is not his mother called Mary? and his brethren, James, and Joses, and Simon, and Judas?* (KJV)

What we are able to conclude is that someone will forge an instrument for the purpose of disrupting or destroying something. Then in the next verse (which is often used incompletely and out of context) Isaiah 54:17, *No weapon that is formed against thee shall prosper; and every tongue that shall rise against thee in judgment thou shalt condemn. This is the heritage of the servants of the Lord, and their righteousness is of me, saith the Lord.* KJV) Nothing that is made on earth will defeat the instrument that will be forged by the one who wields it in righteousness.

Psalm 2:8–9 describes how this instrument forged in fire will be used; *Ask of me, and I shall give thee the heathen for thine inheritance, and the uttermost parts of the earth for thy possession. Thou shalt break them with a rod of iron; thou shalt dash them in pieces like a potter's vessel.* (KJV) Because this has not yet happened in history, we can reason that this is a future event. The one who will receive the authority to do these things will be the one who will be considered יהוה on earth and given the name צדקנו יהוה. (יהוה our righteousness) Jeremiah 23:5–6, *Behold, the days come, saith the LORD, that I will raise unto*

David a righteous Branch, and a King shall reign and prosper, and shall execute judgment and justice in the earth. In his days Judah shall be saved, and Israel shall dwell safely: and this is his name whereby he shall be called, The LORD Our Righteousness. (KJV) This righteous descendent of David will not be יהוה but will act AS יהוה on earth. He will judge and rule righteously until this current earth is destroyed and the new heaven and new earth is created.

Returning to the word *created* in Isaiah 54:16, one should now be able to grasp the reason for the separation between יהוה and ישוע, the one who will be a created servant will be given the authority by יהוה to judge and to rule with a rod of iron on earth but that time has obviously not yet arrived. What the 1st century Pharisees feared was premature. Someone would come to erase their power and authority. The Pharisees were not wrong to look for a leader whom we must hear and obey, they were searching in the wrong time and asking the wrong questions.

Because there are textual variants of the Greek manuscripts, one must remain vigilant and conscious to maintain the continuity from the foundation laid for the New Testament, the Old Testament and in particular the five books of Moses. Any deviation from this foundation weakens the integrity of the entire structure. Many people today are also asking the wrong questions. Because we have inherited lies that have become traditions and led to perverted doctrines we must be deliberate in our quest to find the truth that is found in the sacred word of יהוה.

The political leaders were searching for the righteous king but were afraid they may find him. The religious leaders were searching for *THE PROPHET*, and they too were afraid they may find him. Today Christians have tried to combine the two into one and have created their own confusion. Only when one rejects the polytheistic approach and is able to focus on the individual and their perspective duties and authority are they then able to comprehend the fascinating majestic plan of יהוה.

Isaiah 26:13, ***O LORD*** [יהוה] ***our God, other lords beside thee have had dominion over us: but by thee only will we make mention of thy name.*** (KJV) Only through prayer, repentance and supplication is one able to receive forgiveness of sins and return to the covenant with יהוה. To understand how this process is possible, one needs to understand what a covenant is and how a covenant works.

THE COVENANT

There are three basic components to any covenant:

1. Agreement
2. Arrangent
3. Confirmation

The agreement can be as easy as two or more parties mutually agreeing to be in a covenant relationship. To accomplish this the parties meet together and choose to enter into a covenant. A natural variation of this is for a group to select a representative or a group of representatives to meet in their place as we see in Exodus 19. יהוה spoke to Moses who in turn asked the mixed multitude if they agreed to be in a covenant relationship with יהוה, and the people responded in Exodus 19:8, ***And all the people answered together, and said, All that the LORD hath spoken we will do. And Moses returned the words of the people unto the LORD.*** (KJV)

The arrangement is the parameters of the covenant, what exactly the obligations of each party will be. The arrangement also includes what type of covenant it will be and that in turn dictates the penalties for violating the covenant. (more about that later)

The confirmation of a covenant is more than a signature on a contract, the confirmation is a physical act by both parties. To better explain this the example of a covenant that is used by almost everyone, every day is what is known as a threshold covenant. When someone comes to the entrance of your house and desires to enter, you have a choice. You can allow them access or you can deny them access. By allowing them access you are confirming one half of the covenant, the entering party confirms the second half of the covenant by choosing to enter. The arrangement is practically never discussed because it has become understood though time that the one entering the dwelling will obey the rules established by the owner. In other words you will be a respectful houseguest. If the guest that has been invited into the dwelling becomes unwelcome, the owner has the duty to inform the guest they are in violation of the covenant and if the guest continues to be in violation they must leave as the penalty for violating the covenant. Most people use this covenant without even realizing they have entered into a covenant because in our modern cultures we don't appreciate the recognition of what a covenant really is.

The marriage covenant is somewhat more complicate because it involves an agreement and arrangement between three individuals, the Husband, the wife and יהוה. Once the couple make the decision to be married the agreement is made, they are choosing to be in a covenant of marriage. The arrangement is typically made known in the wedding vows that each person acknowledges to be subject to. The arrangement that יהוה brings is His promise to protect the couple as one family unit, providing them with His instructions for living a healthy, productive, successful and secure life. No marriage has ever failed because יהוה did not keep His promise. When a marriage fails it is alway because one or both humans have violated the parameters outlined in the arrangement and that can include failing to follow the instructions that יהוה provides as His portion of the covenant.

Probably the most familiar covenant spoken of is the blood covenant and it is the most misunderstood as well. Once the parties meet and agree to bond themselves into a covenant relationship, the parameters for the arrangement are made which must be mutually beneficial to each party. To confirm a blood covenant, blood must be shed. The blood can come from either the parties involved themselves or from an animal mutually owned by the parties involved and sacrificed specifically for that purpose. If no animal is owned mutually by both parties then each must bring an adequate animal to sacrifice. The adequacy of the sacrifice is determined by the arrangement and the economic status of the parties involved. The penalty for violating a blood covenant is always the same, the death of the violating party.

Some people through the ages have attempted to equate יהוה clothing Adam and his wife with skins as a blood covenant. There is nothing found in the Bible to indicate a covenant relationship between יהוה and Adam to support this notion. The animals could not have been sacrificed because it was יהוה Himself who provided them, who was יהוה going to sacrifice the animals for; Himself? Because Adam had not seen death at this point, he needed to understand what the result of death is. The lesson Adam learned that day still haunts mankind. Adam being the first created man, did not need to be in a covenant relation-ship with יהוה. The instructions given to Adam in Genesis

2:17, ***But of the tree of the knowledge of good and evil, thou shalt not eat of it: for in the day that thou eatest thereof thou shalt surely die*** (KJV) are not translated well in most Bibles. This translation gives the impression that Adam would die as soon as he ate the fruit but the Hebrew does not give that same impression. Instead it eludes that Adam would begin the process of dying, he wold no longer be an everlasting being on this earth. Being clothed in the skins of the animals impresses upon Adam and his wife the significance of their action.

The covenant between יהוה and Abram in Genesis 15 could be considered a divided or portioned covenant. There is nothing in this passage to indicate this being a blood covenant either. The parameters of the arrangement are portioned as well, this implies that if one part or portion of the covenant is violated not all of the covenant is violated so the penalty is to remove the offending party from that portion of the covenant. When the Israelites violated part of the covenant the exile from the land was the penalty for the violation. Their violation was to ignore allowing the land to rest once every seven years. Jeremiah 25:11, ***And this whole land shall be a desolation, and an astonishment; and these nations shall serve the king of Babylon seventy years.*** (KJV)

Every seven years the land was to rest, known as the sabbatical or Shemitah year. Seven cycles of these years make the Jubilee year. Failing to observe this violated the instructions given to the mixed multitude at Mount sinai in Leviticus 25:3–4, ***Six years thou shalt sow thy field, and six years thou shalt prune thy vineyard, and gather in the fruit thereof; But in the seventh year shall be a sabbath of rest unto the land, a sabbath for the Lord: thou shalt neither sow thy field, nor prune thy vineyard.***

(KJV) Because this instruction is specific to the land it is tied directly to the covenant made with Abram as is the resulting penalty.

The agreement for the blood covenant at Mount Sinai mentioned earlier ushered in the meeting for the arrangement. As יהוה descended on the mountain with all of His majesty and glory, His presence was announced with great fanfare. Exodus 19:16, ***And it came to pass on the third day in the morning, that there were thunders and lightnings, and a thick cloud upon the mount, and the voice of the trumpet exceeding loud; so that all the people that was in the camp trembled.*** (KJV) יהוה introduces Himself in a very formal way that unfortunately does not translate into English well. Exodus 20:2, ***I am the*** [יהוה] ***LORD thy God, which have brought thee out of the land of Egypt, out of the house of bondage.*** (KJV) The formality with which יהוה speaks commands the respect, adoration, honor, fear and every other adjective one could think of when meeting the Creator of the universe.

יהוה Himself would begin to explain the parameters for the arrangement of the covenant. Known to many as the ten commandments and to others as the ten matters, יהוה was interrupted because the people were terrified. The people begged Moses to be their intermediary and speak to יהוה. Exodus 20:19, ***And they said unto Moses, Speak thou with us, and we will hear: but let not God speak with us, lest we die.*** (KJV) What the mixed multitude allowed was for Moses to receive the parameters of the arrangement and they would do whatever Moses said. As Moses went closer to the mountain to be near his Creator, he would need no further assurance from the people. That day Moses sealed his place in Hebrew history as... well none other than... Moses.

Moses received the rest of the arrangement for the covenant that can be found in Exodus chapters 21–23. Then Moses spoke to the people, Exodus 24:3, ***And Moses came and told the people all the words of the Lord, and all the judgments: and all the people answered with one voice, and said, All the words which the Lord hath said will we do.*** (KJV) Next as Moses built an altar and twelve pillars, young men were sent to make burnt offerings and sacrifices to יהוה the blood of the animals was captured because the blood of a sacrifice is never wasted. Half of teh blood Moses sprinkled on the altar to represent יהוה being sprinkled with blood in their presence. What happens next is often overlooked, Exodus 24:7, ***And he took the book of the covenant, and read in the audience of the people: and they said, All that the Lord hath said will we do, and be obedient.*** (KJV) Finally the final event to complete the confirmation of the covenant, after the agreement and arrangement had been finished. Exodus 24:8, ***And Moses took the blood, and sprinkled it on the people, and said, Behold the blood of the covenant, which the Lord hath made with you concerning all these words.*** (KJV) The confirmation of the blood covenant between יהוה and mankind was complete, the one who violated the covenant would die.

Moses returned to the mountain confident that Aaron would be able to manage any trouble that may arise. While Moses stayed on the mountain the people began to think they had been abandoned. Their fears were made known to Aaron and again and again Aaron tried to comfort the people who were certain they had lost their trusted Moses. Even though they had heard יהוה and had seen His voice, the people demanded a god to be in their presence. Aaron negotiated with the men telling them to bring the gold from the ears of their wives and children. Aaron himself melted the gold and made the image of a calf. He made an altar and proclaimed *Here are your gods O Israel tomorrow isa feast to* יהוה. In just a short time, mankind had violated the covenant.

Whatever joy that Moses felt being in the presence of יהוה, was overcome with grief when he heard the anger in the voice of יהוה. Exodus 32:7–8, **And the Lord said unto Moses, Go, get thee down; for thy people, which thou broughtest out of the land of Egypt, have corrupted themselves: They have turned aside quickly out of the way which I commanded them: they have made them a molten calf, and have worshipped it, and have sacrificed thereunto, and said, These be thy gods, O Israel, which have brought thee up out of the land of Egypt.** (KJV)

Moses negotiated between the people and יהוה, finally requesting that he be counted among them and his name be blotted out of the book of life. Exodus 32:32, **Yet now, if thou wilt forgive their sin--; and if not, blot me, I pray thee, out of thy book which thou hast written.** (KJV) The judgement of the people turned from collective to individual at the request of Moses. Exodus 32:33, **And the Lord said unto Moses, Whosoever hath sinned against me, him will I blot out of my book.** (KJV) יהוה would find another way.

As a constant reminder to the people that mankind deserved to die the sacrificial system was implemented by יהוה. Every sin sacrifice that happened was made with the dread of knowing that it was the sinner who deserved to die for violating the covenant. Many years later Paul would write in Hebrew 10:3–4, **But in those sacrifices there is a remembrance again made of sins every year. For it is not possible that the blood of bulls and of goats should take**

away sins. (KJV) The fate of mankind's helplessness and hopelessness appeared to be sealed because of the act of violating the covenant made with יהוה.

Far too many Christians today do not understand the difference between the actual covenant confirmed at Mount Sinai and the punishment necessary for violating the covenant. The parameters of the actual covenant are found in Exodus chapters 20–23. How we are to apply those instructions to our lives are found in the rest of the books Moses right along with the instructions for the sacrifices and the instructions for the priests. The Christian doctrine that the *Law* was done away with is another of the lies we have inherited. The argument for the *Law* to no longer apply comes from a misrepresentation of Paul's writings as neither Paul nor ישוע had the authority to change the instructions given by יהוה. More on this in another chapter.

There are other types of covenants also, the type of covenant, the arrangement and the confirmation may vary depending on the individuals involved. The penalties can be as easy as a simple separation where each party would be free to go their own way or as drastic as requiring the life of the offender. To compare a covenant to a modern contract although there are similarities, the covenant is far more extensive and personal. No one would write a contract to enter a dwelling but the personal involvement in a threshold covenant is far more convenient and binding than a general contract.

The covenant of circumcision should be addressed as it is another of the misunderstood covenants in the Bible. Some have questioned why יהוה would create something that was to be cut off and discarded. The explanation is not as complex as one may imagine but the order of creation needs to be understood. Adam as the first created human was intended to lead, not to dictate, this doesn't mean that he was better than his counterpart or that Eve would be submissive as that came a short time later but left to Adam was the responsibility to set the standard for his household. He would be the first to wake in the morning and begin preparing for the day, Eve would follow his example and begin her daily routine as well. To bring this into today's lifestyle, the man would be the first to begin breakfast with the woman assisting. If the baby's diaper needed to be changed the man didn't wait because it was woman's work, he changed it. When the meal was over the man didn't go read his latest Facebook post, he began washing the dishes. One should shed the idea that man was designed to be better than woman. Male and female are designed to be different while enjoying an interdependent relationship. Of course that intended relationship ended in Genesis 3 when Eve chose to eat the fruit, however יהוה remains unchanging and faithful to His plan.

Genesis 17:11, ***And ye shall circumcise the flesh of your foreskin; and it shall be a token of the covenant betwixt me and you.*** (KJV) Just like everyone born today, the only things that Abraham had when he was born was his life and his body. Asking Abraham to remove a familiar, integral part of the only thing he was born with in an excruciatingly painful and dangerous self inflicted surgical procedure secured his relationship with יהוה. Although in reality it is a small token compared to the promise from יהוה of land and more importantly endless generations of offspring that would include many nations and kings.

This physical sign would mark Abraham and his descendants differently from the rest of the world. By including the following arrangement יהוה offered something to those who were not born of Abraham's children the opportunity to join them in the blessings they receive. Genesis 17:13, *He that is born in thy house, and he that is bought with thy money, must needs be circumcised: and my covenant shall be in your flesh for an everlasting covenant.* (KJV) Notice that the need for circumcision comes *after* becoming part of the household of Abraham. A quick side note needs to be mentioned here that as Paul addressed circumcision in his letters, the Sadducees argued the gentile needed to be circumcised prior to accepting יהוה as their אלהים while Paul stated that faith through believing must come first. Paul's reference to this verse is crucial to understanding his argument for his position.

This covenant is also the foundation for another odd reference in the Bible. Genesis 24:2, *And Abraham said unto his eldest servant of his house, that ruled over all that he had, Put, I pray thee, thy hand under my thigh:* (KJV) The servant in order to take this oath must hold a sacred object, what could be more sacred to Abraham for his most trusted servant to hold than the sign of the covenant between Himself and ייהוה? The extremely important mission the servant was undertaking, to find a suitable wife for Isaac, required the guidance of ייהוה. by taking an oath on the sign of the covenant for Abraham's posterity Abraham was assured that ייהוה would guide his servant to find the right woman for Isaac.

The covenant of circumcision remains as a physical sign among the male population of believers. Even before the mixed multitude left Egypt, the command was given in Exodus 12:48, *And when a stranger shall sojourn with thee, and will keep the passover to the Lord, let all his males be circumcised, and then let him come near and keep it; and he shall be as one that is born in the land: for no uncircumcised person shall eat thereof.* (KJV) One could make the joke that Passover is the most expensive meal a man could ever eat because what it costs him is to be circumcised. Today our modern medical practices have taken circumcision from a sign of the covenant and degraded it to a medical procedure. Even some Jewish people question the need to circumcise their children. The fact remains that for a male to distinguish oneself as being in a covenant relationship with יהוה, circumcision is necessary.

Why does יהוה require a physical sign from men but not from women? Woman was created from man's rib making her a part of him. She receives the breath of life from him and is codependent on him. When a female child is born she is under the umbrella of her father and depends on him as her spiritual covering. The fathers circumcision is the physical sign of the covenant for the family. When a daughter is married that spiritual covering is transferred to the husband. Often asked at modern weddings is *Who gives this woman to be wed?* That question is founded on the transfer of the spiritual covering and should be asked this way, *Who will pass the covering of this woman to this man?* When the father acknowledges this transfer the new family is created and the sign by which that family is part of the covenant is the husband's circumcision because they become one. This is not about ownership of the woman it is about maintaining her covenantal relationship to יהוה.

Because these simple truths have been lost to most modern believers, the traditions and doctrines of men have replaced the truth with the lies we have inherited. The famous Mark Twain is credited with saying, *It is easier to fool a man than to convince him that he has already been fooled.* We seem to enjoy holding on to our traditions even when they can be proven to be a lie because we refuse to admit we have accepted the lies we have inherited from our fathers leaving us confused, worried and trying to force our doctrines into the sacred word of יהוה.

The importance of the covenantal relationships we read about in the Bible are the examples we continue to follow to some degree today. The relationship involved in a covenant helps us recognize how we are to love יהוה with all of our heart, soul, mind and strength and how we are to love our neighbor as one's self. Replacing the covenant relationship with traditions or doctrines founded on the empty lies we have inherited leaves us weak, vulnerable and open to receiving even more lies. Life outside of the covenant with יהוה is a dangerous place but there is hope and protection when we choose to live the way יהוה designed us to live.

PUTTING ALL OF THE PIECES TOGETHER

THERE IS FAR more to Biblical forensics than simply attempting to force verses into a cross reference to form an agenda. Entire passages must conform to complete a narrative or a transcript. Every legitimate passage in the New Testament must continue teaching the lessons gleaned from the instructions in the Old Testament. As explained previously, there are parts of verses in the New Testament and even whole verses that have been added through the centuries (such as John 6:4) that were not part of the original manuscripts.

Many Bible readers today will try to read the Bible as one would read a novel, from beginning to end. The problem in reading the Bible this way is that it is not in chronological order. Found throughout the Bible are lessons recounted from a different perspective. Sometimes when reading the letters of the New Testament we find the writer will include new information not previously included. The gospel of John and the letters attributed to him are good examples of this. Being familiar with John's gospel account and then reading the three epistles of John one can find continuing concepts. Much like someone sending a text today and then sending another because something was left out or needed to be included for clarification.

When we try to piece together the need for the Crucifixion, burial and resurrection, what one discovers is a multipurpose plethora of perplexing information. That may seem confusing, however when one separates ישוע from יהוה and is able to view the servant as someone knit together in the womb for a purpose, then it is possible to comprehend the complex necessity for these things. Isaiah 42:6, ***I the Lord have called thee in righteousness, and will hold thine hand, and will keep thee, and give thee for a covenant of the people, for a light of the Gentiles*** (KJV) How would יהוה accomplish making ישוע a covenant? Without diving into the depth of the Hebrew for the word נתן (na-tahn) translated in this verse as *give thee*, it can also be translated as appoint or set or even deliver. In other words יהוה is delivering someone who will be able to establish (or as one will discover re-establish) the covenant confirmed at Mount Sinai. Remembering the covenant confirmed by blood requires the blood or life of the violating party, only someone who had never violated the covenant would be eligible to pay the price required by the arrangement of the covenant and that the blood of that person would need to be applied to the appropriate alter to satisfy the arrangement as well.

The problem is who would be eligible to make that personal sacrifice and how would the blood (because the blood of a sacrifice is *never* wasted) be applied to an altar that יהוה had established on earth. יהוה in His glorious wisdom arranged for the construction of just such an altar, appropriately named the *Ark Of The Covenant*, complete with the mercy seat, the throne of יהוה on earth. The instructions for constructing the Ark are found in Exodus 25 and there are several variations of artists renderings of what it may look like most of which are incorrect because the artists were not familiar with the original language. The Ark was made to resemble a throne with the Cherubim standing on each end facing inward with a wing stretched across to form the back of the throne and the other wing outstretched upward. The poles used to carry the Ark were long enough to ensure stability when moving the Ark and remained in place after it was eventually put in place in the Temple known as the *The Most Holy Place*. 2 Chronicles 5:7, ***And the priests brought in the ark of the covenant of the LORD unto his place, to the oracle of the house, into the most holy place, even under the wings of the cherubim*** (KJV)

The Ark remained in *The Most Holy Place* until Nebuchadnezzar destroyed the first Temple. 2 Maccabees 2:5–7, *Jeremiah came and found a cave-dwelling, and he brought there the tent and the ark and the altar of incense; then he sealed up the entrance. Some of those who followed him came up intending to mark the way, but could not find it. When Jeremiah learned of it, he rebuked them and declared: "The place shall remain unknown until God gathers his people together again and shows his mercy.* This passage records Jeremiah as he one who actually was overseeing the hiding of the Ark in an underground cave in Jerusalem. He also made certain that no markings were to be carved into the rock to give any clue as to the whereabouts of the Ark. To this day there is much disputed controversy and speculation about where the Ark currently is.

Peter writes that ישוע is the example that we should follow. 1 Peter 2:21–22, ***That is what you were called to*** *do. Christ suffered for you. He gave you an example to follow. So you should do as he did. "He did no sin He never lied."* (ICB) Peter is practically quoting Isaiah 53:9, *He was buried like a criminal, but in a rich man's grave; but he had done no wrong and had never spoken an evil word.* (TLB) John and Paul both agree with Peter that ישוע never once violated the any of the instructions from יהוה, but he insisted that people should follow the word of יהוה instead of the rules of men. This example and even his teaching entitle ישוע to be eligible for the sacrifice that pays the debt of blood we owe to יהוה for mankind's violation of the covenant confirmed at Mount Sinai. So how was יהוה able to ensure the blood of ישוע was not wasted if he was the perfect sacrifice?

John's narrative of the crucifixion is an eye witness account of the event. Beginning in chapter 18, John gives in exhausting detail the play-by- play details of the arrest, trial and brutal crucifixion. John was standing with Mary as ישוע charges John with her future care saying *Woman behold your son.* John was standing close enough to see, hear and feel the earth move and split even though he doesn't record that. John was close enough to watch the soldier pierce the side of ישוע and to see the blood and water spill from his body. Then John suddenly stops the narration and in verse 35 we read, *And he that saw it bare record, and his record is true: and he knoweth that he saith true, that ye might believe.* (KJV) What did John see that was so incredible, so unexpected and so miraculous that he would write, *I'm writing this so there is a record?* What was so important that it could not be included in as much detail in his account?

Later John would write his first letter, 1 John 5:8, *And there are three that bear witness in earth, the Spirit, and the water, and the blood: and these three agree in one.*

(KJV) Could John have been the only witness to something so important that he could only allude to what he had seen? Did John actually see the blood and water spill through a split in the ground caused by the earthquake an onto something spectacular? Did John witness the perfect redemption payment for our violation of the covenant as the blood poured onto the mercy seat? The only alter worthy of being used as the doorpost for mankind; to anoint the blood of the sacrifice to pay the debt we owe?

The day ישוע was crucified was not Yom Kippur, it was only hours before the Passover was to be eaten. Had the [perfect] lamb been sacrificed so that the death angel would pass over us until the confirmation was able to renew the covenant at a future event?

To understand these questions one should be familiar with what are known as the Biblical feasts found in Leviticus 23. These appointed times are mentioned in Hebrews 10:1, ***The law is only an unclear picture of the good things coming in the future. It is not a perfect picture of the real things. The people under the law offered the same sacrifices every year. These sacrifices can never make perfect those who come near to worship God.*** (ICB) These *unclear* or shadow pictures represent the underlying meanings of the weekly and annual events. The most Holy day of the year for the Hebrew people is Yom Kippur, the Day of Atonement. On this day the High Priest would enter the *Most Holy Place* and sprinkle blood on the mercy seat. The blood of a bull was to be used for the sins of the priest and his family but the blood of a kid goat was to be used to cover the sins of the people. He was to sprinkle the blood seven times with his finger toward the East side of the mercy seat. These very strict instructions can be found in Leviticus 16. No description of ישוע ever connects him with a goat, he is described as the lamb, John 1:29, ***The next day John seeth Jesus coming unto him, and saith, Behold the Lamb of God, which taketh away the sin of the world.*** (KJV) While our current understanding of this translation may not be exactly what John actually said, it's close enough to know he didn't not say *kid goat* or *bull.* The textual variants of this verse read, *Behold* אלהים *carries the sin of the world.*

The significance of a lamb without blemish at Passover is far different than the goats for Yom Kippur. The lamb must live in your house and be inspected thoroughly. The lamb must be sacrificed properly with the blood captured and used to cover the doorposts of the house. This was done so the angel of death would pass over the home. The necessity for the blood of the lamb instead of a goat to be poured onto the mercy seat at Passover instead of Yom Kippur must have extremely relevant meaning. There is no physical door for humanity, anointing the Mercy seat with the blood of ישוע is a physical representation of Moses sprinkling blood on the altar at Mount Sinai. This event ushers in the ability to begin the journey from the bondage of the sacrificial system of sin offerings to a renewing of the covenant with יהוה.

Paul writes in detail that the ultimate sacrifice for sin has been made in Hebrew 9–10. Hebrew 10:3–4 ***But in those sacrifices there is a remembrance again made of sins every year. For it is not possible that the blood of bulls and of goats should take away sins.*** (KJV) The animal sacrifices were our constant reminder that blood must be paid in blood. Payment for payment. Paul writes that ישוע intercedes between mankind and יהוה, (Hebrews 9:15) because where the covenant is violated there must be retribution. The renewal of the covenant will be confirmed at a future event commonly known as the marriage supper of the lamb.

The covenant was always available to the gentiles, first revealed in Exodus 12:49, ***One law shall be to him that is homeborn, and unto the stranger that sojourneth among you.*** (KJV) Then again in Numbers 15:16 and in Numbers 15:29. The Hebrew word for *law* in these verses is תורה, Torah, typically defined as instructions and this has always included the books of Moses, the first five books of the Old Testament. Following the Exile and then the Greek and Roman occupation one is able to see through the writings of that time, a distinct separation of Jew and gentile was established. The former inclusion of the gentiles was replaced with a desire for revenge against the oppressors thus creating a feeling of contempt for the children of Abraham. The religious rulers of the 2nd century BC began introducing different rules for the people who chose to accept the אלהים of Abraham, these became known as the Noahide laws. These Noahide laws maintained the separation between Jew and gentile ignoring the Torah instruction that there was only one law to become a bonafide member of the Creator's family. The blood of ישוע as the final and perfect redemption sacrifice reopens the covenant to everyone who would choose to place their trust in יהוה, something that was evidently lost to the early church.

Paul is very careful in his epistle to the Hebrews to not make the blood of ישוע any type of covering for our sin but to prove ישוע as the intercessor on our behalf allowing everyone who chooses to live according to the torah, the instructions from יהוה, to be welcomed fully into His family providing they agree to live according to those instructions.

One is now challenged to consider that if ישוע is the final sacrifice to repay mankind debt of blood, making the covenant free, what will be the final sacrifice for sin itself? During the fall feast of Yom Kippur two kid goats were brought to the Tabernacle and eventually to the Temple. Lots were cast and one goat was to be sacrificed with it's blood sprinkled seven times on the mercy seat, the other was to be put out into the wilderness. Leviticus 16:9–10, ***And Aaron shall bring the goat upon which the LORD's lot fell, and offer him for a sin offering. But the goat, on which the lot fell to be the scapegoat, shall be presented alive before the LORD, to make an atonement with him, and to let him go for a scapegoat into the wilderness.*** (KJV) By chasing the scapegoat out of the camp or away from the people we are reminded that sin exists in the world. The tradition became that the scapegoat would be chased off and driven over a cliff to his death. By killing the scapegoat, the shadow picture is destroyed and gives mankind the idea that man can overcome and kill sin without the aid of יהוה.

What do each of these goats represent? The sacrificial goat is a foreshadow for the man who would represent evil in the world. Commonly known as the antichrist this man is mentioned several times in the Bible. Beginning in 2 Thessalonians 2:3–4, ***Let no man deceive you by any means: for that day shall not come, except there come a falling away first, and that man of sin be revealed, the son of perdition; Who opposeth and exalteth himself above all that is called God, or that is worshipped; so that he as God sitteth in the temple of God, shewing himself that he is God.*** (KJV) Make no mistake that this man will not only speak against יהוה but will attempt to raise himself above every other god known to mankind. His time will be short as we learn in verse 8, ***And then shall that Wicked be revealed, whom the LORD shall consume with the spirit of his mouth, and shall destroy with*** *the brightness of his coming:* (KJV) This is confirmed in Daniel 8:25, ***And through his policy also he shall cause craft to prosper in his hand; and he shall magnify himself in his heart, and by peace shall destroy many: he shall also stand up against the Prince of princes; but he shall be broken without [human] hand.*** (KJV) If this man of perdition or sorrow is seated in the Temple one should understand he will be sitting on the Ark of the Covenant. When יהוה speaks and destroys the man of sorrow his blood will be on the mercy seat, completing the earthly fall feast of Yom Kippur. Payment for payment.

The *scapegoat*, represents a group of people, Leviticus 16, 21–22, ***And Aaron shall lay both his hands upon the head of the live goat, and confess over him all the iniquities of the children of Israel, and all their transgressions in all their sins, putting them upon the head of the goat, and shall send him away by the hand of a fit man into the wilderness: And the goat shall bear upon him all their iniquities unto a land not inhabited: and he shall let go the goat in the wilderness.*** (KJV) Those who will still choose to rebel against יהוה, they will be forced out of the camp, away form the fellowship of believers. Eventually they will face the final death in the lake of fire after the final judgement. They have blotted their names from the book of life.

The death of ישוע not only provides the blood for the sacrifice, his death provides the imagery necessary to reveal another level of satisfaction for the spring feasts. As ישוע was prepared for burial this action was similar to the lamb being made ready for the oven. Of course the lamb would be roasted and ready later that evening while ישוע would remain in the tomb. When the Sadducees asked for a sign ישוע replied this way in Matthew 12:39–40, ***But he*** *answered and said unto them, An evil and adulterous generation seeketh after a sign; and there shall no sign be given to it, but the sign of the prophet Jonas: For as Jonas was three days and three nights in the whale's belly; so shall the Son of man be three days and three nights in the heart of the earth.* (KJV) He was able to speak this by the authority of being *THE PROPHET*—Deuteronomy 18:18, *I will raise them up a Prophet from among their brethren, like unto thee, and will put my words in his mouth; and he shall speak unto them all that I shall command him.* (KJV) ישוע wasn't speaking of his own words, he was speaking what was given to him. Consider the reason that יהוה would provide a fish, born most likely many years before Jonah to be large enough to provide a place of refuge for Jonah. A place where Jonah would repent and pray, a place that seemed so strange and different to him. The belly of the fish was for Jonah a place where he didn't really change his heart, he still didn't like the people of Nineveh but he went on to complete his assignment. Jonah understood that יהוה will stop at nothing to save as many souls as possible.

The death of ישוע as a human being also displays that our now fallen state of humanity that is no longer perfect must be transformed, this transformation can not occur in this fallen and cursed world. Remember that only this this earth was weakened by יהוה as He orders the punishment for mankind. Although the entire physical universe is effected. Romans 8:22, *For we know that the whole creation groaneth and travaileth in pain together until now.* (KJV) Paul writes that all of creation feels the pain of sin. All of creation realizes that eventually everything must be destroyed so that it can be remade perfect once again. ישוע understood this as well when he chose to be faithful unto his death, knowing that even he would be remade, perfect once again. That is our example to follow, remaining faithful and being the example to the people around us, living the way our Creator, יהוה, designed us to live until our assignment on this earth is completed and we go on to be remade, perfect and able to be in the presence of יהוה.

If the death of ישוע is our example that all of creation must be destroyed, how much greater this is to know that the resurrection can allow us to be remade, perfect. Remembering the Sadducees failure to acknowledge the possibility of the resurrection, their lack of hope must be devastating. One may wonder why their focus on civil regulation revolved around the political world they lived in. Without the possibility of eternal life, all we are left with is what we have in our immediate presence.

The difference between modern Christians and the sadducees is the Christian focus only on eternity and the Sadducees focus is on the current situation. Both neglect the necessity to include a balance of both. Many Christian denominations that teach eternal life in heaven, allow for sin after confession and faith in Jesus. Their doctrine fails to include the simple edict that we must sin no more. The sadducee doctrine was that it was sin not to follow their civil rules. The people the sadducees were ruling understood sin, their hope was for someone to come and free them from their oppression, what they received was someone to free them from the oppression of hopelessness. יהוה sent ישוע to teach that the man made rules and even the rules of the Pharisees were useless to enter the kingdom of heaven. Instead ישוע as *THE PROPHET* taught his followers to obey the instructions יהוה gave to mankind through Moses.

The resurrection of ישוע provided hope to the hopeless. The men, women and children who witnessed the events in Israel during the early part of the 1st century experienced יהוה actively working in their lifetime. They watched as יהוה Himself supplied the proof of eternal life, fulfilling His promise that we can always trust Him. The Sadducees, afraid of losing their rule were offended by this heavenly display of love. They chose to persecute the people who accepted hope in a land that was occupied by foreign oppressors. As the first followers of ישוע rejected the man made regulations of the Pharisees, the Sadducees were terrified these people would soon rebel against Rome and cause the destruction of Israel. But is wasn't the hopeful who caused the fall of Israel and the destruction of the Temple, it was the hopeless.

While the Pharisees were sending out men like Paul to find, persecute and kill the disciples of ישוע, they were causing a disruption with the day to day business of Roman rule. The Roman rulers had no choice but to completely destroy any form of Jewish government in order to secure complete Roman sovereignty. There were several factions of Jewish infighting as well, however the main source was indeed the lust of the Pharisees to remain in control of the people.

The hope that we have today is not about sitting on a cloud in heaven playing a harp. The hope delivered through the resurrection assures us that as ישוע is our example to follow, we will be resurrected in our due time. Paul writes in 1 Corinthians 15:22–23, ***For as in Adam all die, even so in Christ shall all be made alive. But every man in his own order: Christ, the firstfruits; afterward they that are Christ's at his coming.*** (KJV) For those who rejected יהוה their resurrection will be just before the judgement described in Revelation 20:11–15, And I saw a great white throne, and him that sat on it, from whose face the earth and the heaven fled away; and there was found no place for them. And I saw the dead, small and great, stand before God; and the books were opened: and another book was opened, which is the book of life: and the dead were judged out of those things which were written in the books, according to their works. And the sea gave up the dead which were in it; and death and hell delivered up the dead which were in them: and they were judged every man according to their works. And death and hell were cast into the lake of fire. This is the second death. And whosoever was not found written in the book of life was cast into the lake of fire. (KJV)

Everyone will at some time in the future be resurrected, for those who choose יהוה as their אלהים they will be remade perfect once again. For those who reject יהוה, they will certainly die the second death, never to be remembered. Our hope in the resurrection and having the opportunity to be reunited with יהוה and to stand in His presence just as Adam did is only part of the glory to which believers look forward. Reading about what the new heaven and new earth will be like including the new Jerusalem, not just in Revelation but throughout the prophets brings an indescribable joy to the spirit of believers.

Together the death, burial and resurrection is a symbol of love and hope. They are only part of the complex and wonderful plan that יהוה has to make His creation perfect once again. Some denominations attempt to force the death, burial and resurrection to be the gospel message but that is not accurate. The death, burial and resurrection are vitally important but the gospel message that was once delivered to the saints is different. The gospel that ישוע spoke is found in Matthew 4:17, ***From that time Jesus began to preach, and to say, Repent: for the kingdom of heaven is at hand.*** (KJV) The real gospel message is found all over the Old Testament, Confess your sin and repent, the kingdom of יהוה is very close. The phrase *at hand* gives the impression that if you stretch your hand as far as you can, the kingdom would be just past the tip of your finger. That is how close it is and that is how far away it is too. Imagine understanding that יהוה is that close to you, not close enough to touch Him because we are in the process of dying physically but close enough that He will hear our barely audible prayer.

For the unfortunate Christian who only hears trust Jesus and he will solve all your problems, they are missing the greatest blessings that יהוה is waiting to pour over them. Failing to live the way we are designed to live and following the instructions from יהוה, we deny ourselves the complete relationship He desires to have with us.

Contrary to popular belief, יהוה does not love us all the same, Psalm 5:5, ***Those people who make fun of you cannot stand before you. You hate all those who do wrong.*** (ICB) Yes, יהוה reserves the right to hate anyone who chooses to deny He is real or chooses a life of evil. On the other hand, repeated in His sacred word is this theme first found in Exodus 19:5, ***Now therefore, if ye will obey my voice indeed, and keep my covenant, then ye shall be a peculiar treasure unto me above all people: for all the earth is mine:*** (KJV) What makes us a special treasure? When we choose יהוה. Leviticus 26:12, ***I will walk among you and be your God, and you will be My people.*** (KJV) And repeated in Jeremiah 7:23, ***But this thing commanded I them, saying, Obey my voice, and I will be your God, and ye shall be my people: and walk ye in all the ways that I have commanded you, that it may be well unto you.*** (KJV) Then repeated two more times in Jeremiah to impress the importance of this concept.

As important as the death, burial and resurrection are, they are less important than the obedience יהוה demands from us. The inadvertent violation is easily repaired with prayer and repentance but the deliberate denial of יהוה or the rejection of His instructions for self centered purposes is evil and will result in the final death because you have blotted out your name from His book of life. יהוה is the אלהים of the living. When ישוע was asked about marriage in heaven, his response from Mark 12:24–27, *And Jesus answering said unto them, Do ye not therefore err, because ye know not the scriptures, neither the power of God? For when they shall rise from the dead, they neither marry, nor are given in marriage; but are as the angels which are in heaven. And as touching the dead, that they rise: have ye not read in the book of Moses, how in the bush God spake unto him, saying, I am the God of Abraham, and the God of Isaac, and the God of Jacob? He is not the God of the dead, but the God of the living: ye therefore do greatly err.* (KJV)

When ישוע was speaking to someone who wanted to follow him but wanted to bury his father he said this in Matthew 12:22, *But Jesus said unto him, Follow me; and let the dead bury their dead.* (KJV) He isn't speaking about someone who has physically died being able to bury someone, he is saying, *Let those who don't believe take care of themselves!* Those who choose not to follow the instructions of יהוה are considered by ישוע to be unbelievers. They do not enjoy the blessings of יהוה nor should they. יהוה may work His miracles to deliver the message to you but what you choose to do with the information is your decision.

The shadow pictures we have been given in the books of Moses are found primarily in the feasts but there is a shadow picture that was never allowed to be destroyed, the blessing used when bread and wine are served. Before eating bread, the blessing is;

**blessed are you, יהוה, ourour אלהים
King of the universe, who brings forth
bread form the earth**

Notice in this blessing the bread is not blessed, יהוה is the one we bless. This is the blessing we read about in the accounts of the last supper. ישוע never blessed the bread or the wine, he spoke the same blessing that has been embedded in the Hebrew culture since Abraham heard this same blessing from the righteous king, Melchizedek. (Not his name but his title) Abraham was so overcome that he offered 10% of all he owned to the king and then he taught this blessing to his family and his servants and it has not changed since that time.

The few short words in Hebrew and the simple expression in English can not come close to describing everything that is encompassed in this blessing. Here is one way to describe what the blessing actually holds;

*The first house (Heaven) will allow a powerful
sign to reveal a great work, behold יהוה will be
your security. Look and see! יהוה's instructions
reveal mighty works through his son and his life
will be made open. Look and know the son will
teach how you should live.*

*Behold life is a journey, obey the most high and
bind your earthly life to the life of the son of
Yahovah. See, He is powerful, the first from the
beginning and He will be your shepherd.*

This is how Abraham may have understood the blessing of the bread. Then he heard the righteous king bless יהוה while holding the wine as an example;

Blessed are you יהוה, our אלהים King of the universe, creator of the fruit of the vine

Imagine hearing this for the first time and in your mind you understand it this way;

The house of יהוה is the first and most powerful.
יהוה will scatter those who first worshipped Him
but look! יהוה will gather the scattered to
His son.

Still today, every Jewish person will speak these blessings before bread is eaten or wine is brought to the lips. Some may not understand the importance of the blessing today in this manner and yet these shadow pictures are so important they have lasted almost 4,000 years without being completely destroyed.

Although יהוה has allowed us to inherit lies, He protects his promise to Abraham in this unassuming blessing. The children of Abraham will be gathered together by יהוה Himself.

BUT PAUL SAID

WANT TO BEGIN an argument? Start a sentence with, *But Paul said.* Paul or שאול (Sha-ool or saul) is credited with writing much of the New Testament. Most people will misquote what Peter had to say about Paul. 2 Peter 3:16, **As also in all his epistles, speaking in them of these things; in which are some things hard to be understood, which they that are unlearned and unstable wrest, as they do also the other scriptures, unto their own destruction.** (KJV) Peter doesn't write that Paul is difficult to understand. Peter writes that Paul writes of things or maters that are difficult to understand *IF* one is unwise or unstable or fails to comprehend other scripture. According to Peter, people have been twisting scripture for a very long time.

When one is familiar with the Old Testament, most of the things Paul writes should also be familiar. In other words Paul constantly quotes from the Old Testament! Paul had no reason to change anything and was smart enough to know he did not have the authority to change any of the instructions from יהוה. Even though Paul was from the tribe of Benjamin, Philippians 3:5, **Circumcised the eighth day, of the stock of Israel, of the tribe of Benjamin, an**

Hebrew of the Hebrews; as touching the law, a Pharisee. (KJV) He describes himself as a zealot for the law of Moses.

During the second Temple period someone aspiring to be a Pharisee would need to memorize the Torah, the first five books of the Old Testament. The test would be verbal, an instructor would begin with a word or phrase and the student would then be expected to recite what Moses had written until he was told to stop. This meant that if the teacher began with *In the beginning,* the student would continue until he was instructed to stop or he reached the end of Deuteronomy, without hesitation or mistake. This is how well Paul understood the Law and he was practically equal in his knowledge of the prophets as well.

Paul would never violate what he held so dear. Deuteronomy 4:2, *Ye shall not add unto the word which I command you, neither shall ye diminish ought from it, that ye may keep the commandments of the Lord your God which I command you.* (KJV) Please remember this important detail:

PAUL DOES NOT HAVE THE AUTHORITY TO CHANGE THE SACRED WORD OF יהוה

Not even ישוע dared to change anything that יהוה had given in His word. Matthew 5:17–19, *Think not that I am come to destroy the law, or the prophets: I am not come to destroy, but to fulfil. For verily I say unto you, Till heaven and earth pass, one jot or one tittle shall in no wise pass from the law, till all be fulfilled. Whosoever therefore shall break one of these least commandments, and shall teach men so, he shall be called the least in the kingdom of heaven: but whosoever shall do and teach*

them, the same shall be called great in the kingdom of heaven. (KJV) To destroy the law would be to add to it or diminish from it. Those who would claim that Paul changed any aspect of what was written are placing more importance on Paul than on ישוע who they claim is their lord. This inconsistent behavior comes from the polytheistic mindset that one can place their faith where it is convenient.

Everything that Paul writes confirms what was written by Moses or the other writers of the Old Testament. He never once attempts to change anything, anyone who believes that Paul has changed what he believed with all of his heart, mind and soul is part of the unlearned or unstable that Peter writes about. There are no contradictions in the Bible. Any time we find something that seems to be a contradiction, it is because we don't understand what is being written. The contradiction belongs to the reader, not the writer. The responsibility to satisfy the perceived contradiction falls to the reader. Understanding that most contradiction are from mistranslations is a good place to begin, then move through the process of confirming if it is a translation problem or was something added or deleted to help uphold an agenda.

Several denominations have developed doctrines founded on a misunderstanding or misinterpretation of Pauls writings. One could consider the crass doctrine that the law was nailed to the cross is the most damaging doctrine of the Christian world. This doctrine is based on Collisions 2:14, ***Blotting out the handwriting of ordinances that was against us, which was contrary to us, and took it out of the way, nailing it to his cross;*** (KJV) Rather than jump to the irrational conclusion the handwritten ordinances are the first five books of the Bible and forgetting about the

Matthew 5:17 passage, an effort should be made to find out where the hand written accusation would be found to which Paul is referring.

John 19:17–21, *Carrying his own cross, Jesus went out to a place called The Place of the Skull. (In the Jewish language this place is called Golgotha.) 18 There they nailed Jesus to the cross. They also put two other men on crosses, one on each side of Jesus with Jesus in the middle. 19 Pilate wrote a sign and put it on the cross. It read: "JESUS OF NAZARETH, THE KING OF THE JEWS." 20 The sign was written in the Jewish language, in Latin, and in Greek. Many of the Jews read the sign, because this place where Jesus was killed was near the city. 21 The leading Jewish priests said to Pilate, "Don't write, 'The King of the Jews.' But write, 'This man said, I am the King of the Jews.'" Pilate answered, "What I have written, I have written!" (ICB) This should be self explanatory however most translations fail to accurately reflect what Paul had written in the Colossians 2:14 verse.*

Luke 16:29–31, *But Abraham said, 'They have the law of Moses and the writings of the prophets to read; let them learn from them!' 30 The rich man said, 'No, father Abraham! If someone came to them from the dead, they would believe and change their hearts and lives.' 31 But Abraham said to him, 'No! If your brothers won't listen to Moses and the prophets, then they won't listen to someone who comes back from death.* (ICB) In this parable ישוע is extremely assertive that everyone must listen to Moses and the prophets and do what is written. Using anything that Paul had written to devalue or negate anything in the old Testament is useless as Paul continually quotes from or refers to the Old Testament to verify and clarify what he is writing about.

When studying the Bible we find evidence of some things that were added. This is especially true of the New Testament. One easy way to determine if something suspicious was added is to find a witness in the Old Testament. If there are no cross references than the chances are it was added to the Bible. Another way is to read the passage carefully and ask if it reads exactly like the writer had been writing. In other words does it sound like the surrounding writing? This is extremely evident in Matthew 28:19, **Go ye therefore, and teach all nations, baptizing them in the name of the Father, and of the Son, and of the Holy Ghost:** (KJV) Nowhere else does ישוע refer to himself this way and Matthew doesn't write this way in his narrative. Keep these things in mind when studying Paul's epistles.

Paul has a way of writing that is unmistakably Hebrew and it shows in the Greek, in the English and probably every other language to which it has been translated. The textual variants of Paul's epistles are many, some can be attributed to simply copying the originals by hand repeatedly. Other variations are credited to the scribes using notes in the margins and then the notes are eventually moved into the body of the text by a later scribe. There is much speculation to exactly how much of Romans 13 was actually written by Paul. There are passages in the Old Testament to support being obedient to a king but Paul's actions do not reflect this writing. While in Damascus Paul escapes the authority of the governor. Acts 9:24–25, **But their laying await was known of Saul. And they watched the gates day and night to kill him. Then the disciples took him by night, and let him down by the wall in a basket.** (KJV) One should be critical of these passages when one thing is written but the writers action is not consistent with what they are credited for writing.

Bear in mind, these discrepancies are not contradictions in the sacred word of יהוה, these are contradictions added by man. Paul lived among the Corinthians for almost two years. In that time it is reasonable to believe that if women should physically cover their heads with a hat or scarf he would have addressed it at the time. There was no need to wait and write to them about something he had ample opportunity to resolve while he was with them. 1 Corinthians 11:5, ***But every woman that prayeth or prophesieth with her head uncovered dishonoureth her head: for that is even all one as if she were shaven.*** (KJV) Some modern denominations require women to wear some type of head covering because this passage is not only mistranslated it is misunderstood.

One could successfully argue that the 1 Corinthians 11 chapter is more proof that the entire epistle was written in Hebrew based only one word, ראש, (rosh) meaning head or source. First used in Genesis 2:10 to describe the headwaters or source of the rivers flowing out of Eden, this word like many has more than one possible definition. What Paul is explaining to the Corinthians is that the source of the woman is man because woman is created from Adam's rib. And the source of man is ישוע because he is the one who has made to possible for us to be free from the sacrificial system. The source of ישוע is יהוה who also created him. Paul is writing to them about the order of creation, not to degrade or devalue women through a hierarchy society but so they all understand the way יהוה has designed His the order of relationships in His creation.

Of notable significance, the epistles Paul are credited with writing are not in Chronological order. While there is some debate and speculation as to the exact chronology of the entire New Testament. Many scholars believe that Paul was writing long before the disciples had written their gospel accounts. We also know that not all of Paul's epistles are included. 1Corinthians 5:9, ***I wrote unto you in an epistle not to company with fornicators:*** (KJV) According to this verse Paul had written a prior letter, one that is not included.

There is evidence that Pauls first epistles were to the Thessalonians, and then to the Galatians. As Paul was traveling and writing he is also meeting with some of the disciples. One needs to be aware of the speculation surrounding the chronology of the writing because if Paul's writing's come before the gospels, then the gospels could have been written to clarify Paul. The disciples had information about the life and teaching of ישוע that Paul was not familiar with, although Paul had intricate knowledge of the Torah, the writing of Moses, that the disciples were not as familiar with.

The most agreed chronological order of Pauls epistles seems to be:

1 Thessalonians, 2 Thessalonians
Galatians
1 Corinthians, 2 Corinthians
Romans
Philemon
Colossians
Ephesians
Philippians
1 Timothy
Titus
2 Timothy

Hebrews is a unique book that causes one to question who the author is. While most believe Paul wrote Hebrews, some believe that Peter is the actual author. The list of textual variants in Hebrews is quite long and there are places that it does read as if some verses could have been added, most differences can be attributed to copying error. The writer had a great knowledge of the Torah and prophets which suggests Paul and not Peter as the writer. In our modern minds we enjoy the thought that the disciples were men and women of great Biblical knowledge. The reality is they were not highly educated people. Fishermen, tax collector, and simple everyday folks. Paul is the one who had the technical background of scripture but the disciples had the teaching of ישוע.

Because Paul's writing is the majority of the New Testament, the opportunity for additions and mistakes in translations is increased. Because the sacred word of יהוה can not hold any contradictions Paul could not give one set of instructions to one group and a separate set of instructions to another. In this same way Paul could not say that the blood of ישוע keeps us safe from the wrath of יהוה in Romans 5:9, ***Much more then, being now justified by his blood, we shall be saved from wrath through him.*** KJV) Then write something different to the Ephesians in 1:7, ***In whom we have redemption through his blood, the forgiveness of sins, according to the riches of his grace;*** (KJV)

The Romans verse is consistent with the lesson from Exodus. The blood of the lamb protects us from the wrath of יהוה, in the event of Exodus it was the death angel. That allowed the children of Abraham the freedom to go to Mount Sinai and meet with יהוה. There were not made righteous by the blood of the lamb, they were freed to pursue righteousness by the good of the lamb. that is exactly what Paul writes to the Romans. The Ephesians verse that we currently have appears to change the purpose of the blood, or does it?

One needs to understand the definition of redemption when the Bible was translated into English. Noah Webster's 1828 American Dictionary of the English Language begins the first definition of redemption as the *repurchase of captured goods.* This concept fits perfectly when we consider the blood of the lambs at the first Passover in Egypt paid the price of blood to anoint the doorposts. The blood protected or paid the price to keep the firstborn safe inside. The good of ישוע pays again for the protection of not just the firstborn but everyone who chooses יהוה as their אלהים. Paul better than the scribes who copied his letters or the editors who promote their agendas today that the blood of a lamb in the spring of the year was not the shadow picture of a sin sacrifice. יהוה demands life for life, eye for eye tooth for tooth. Payment for payment. Sin must shed blood for sin. Only the blood of someone who had never violated the covenant is eligible to repurchase the covenant. Payment for payment. Only the blood of the truly rebellious the evil one can make the final sin sacrifice. Payment for payment.

Pauls knowledge and zeal for the Torah and the prophets made him the ideal person to carry the message of a monotheistic form of worship into a polytheistic world. Those who have corrupted his epistles are guilty of far more than artistic license. Even Pauls use of the word scripture has been redefined to include his own writing. 2 Timothy 3:16, ***All scripture is given by inspiration of God, and is profitable for doctrine, for reproof, for correction, for instruction in righteousness:*** (KJV) Today we consider the things that Paul wrote as scripture. Paul may argue that concept. When we think of the probability that Paul was writing his epistles before the gospels had been written down, what Paul refers to as scripture is found in our Old Testament. Many modern denominations refuse the Old

Testament, replacing it with a perverse interpretation of Paul's writing. According to Paul, when this happens there is no sound doctrine, blame, correction or instruction.

How can one expect to understand what Paul writes if the very thing that Paul writes about is rejected? Paul was well aware the Jeremiah warned us of inheriting lies, that may be one reason Paul goes into such detail in his epistles. Paul's desire for the truth to be known is evident, our understanding of his detail pitifully falls short of expectation. Yet for the tenacious, there are pearls of glorious wisdom in Paul's writing that can only be appreciated when knowing from where he draws his conclusions. The single thing that makes Paul so brilliant is that he realizes how little he knows. Paul constantly refers back to what he considers scripture to be and quotes it or paraphrases it a majority of the time. When someone blurts out, *But Paul said*, what they are about to repeat, unless it is corrupted, will come from somewhere in the Old Testament.

RIGHTEOUSNESS IS AN OBLIGATION

Holiness does not necessarily equal righteousness, unless your name is יהוה. Noah is the first person in the Bible described as righteous, Genesis 6:9, *These are the generations of Noah. Noah was a righteous man, and perfect in his generations: Noah walked with God.* (ASV) Noah is also described as walking with אלהים. Abram on the other hand was ninety-nine years old and his faith challenged often when יהוה instructs Abram to walk in His presence. Genesis 17:1 *And when Abram was ninety years old and nine, the Lord appeared to Abram, and said unto him, I am the Almighty God; walk before me, and be thou perfect.* (KJV)

Deuteronomy 13:4, *Ye shall walk after the LORD your God, and fear him, and keep his commandments, and obey his voice, and ye shall serve him, and cleave unto him.* (KJV) What does the phrase *walk after* אלהים יהוה really mean? Some believe it to be a friendly relationship and use the example of people walking on a journey together. This example may give the illusion of getting to know the each other but יהוה knits us together, He already knows us intimately. A better example would be to think of mankind as an apprentice. Made on the image of יהוה, we are to learn how to be more like Him. Our *job* so to speak is not to just be a friend of יהוה, we are to learn from Him. We learn His ways so that we can become more like Him.

During the time between Noah and Moses, mankind experienced an event that severely affected the Spiritual relationship with יהוה. The events on the plains of Shinar, were more injurious for mankind than simply confusing the language. Noah's perfection was not passed along to his sons. Shem was able to observe his father's faith and dedication through his obedience to יהוה, something that may have been tossed to Ham and Japeth. There is more than legend that suggests Shem is the righteous king Melchizedek) who visited Abraham. Shem was the oldest living patriarch in the line of the promised seed prior to Abraham and actually outlived Abraham.

Because of the trust that Abraham's ancestors placed in יהוה, he was on the perfect position for יהוה to call him out of the land of his father. Remember that Abraham was not considered perfect until after he had been trusting יהוה for many years, he was probably younger than seventy five years old when he first heard the Creator's voice. Abram's choice to trust יהוה begins the in depth detailed history of humanity. Prior to Genesis chapter 12 the Bible contains a general overview of Creation and the flood of Noah but only selected highlight of important events and people. After the introduction of Abram, Moses really begins to detail the lives of the people and places involved along with the way that יהוה gives direction to His chosen people.

Leviticus 11:44, ***For I am the LORD your God; consecrate yourselves, therefore, and be holy, because I*** *am holy. You must not defile yourselves by any creature that crawls along the ground.* (BSB) The first time the word Holy is used in the Bible (in this context) is found in Exodus 3:5, *And he said, Draw not nigh hither: put off thy shoes from off thy feet, for the place whereon thou standest is holy ground.* (KJV) The root word for holy is קדש (kōděsh) and is defined as being set apart. This is original intended purpose for the mixed multitude that came out of Egypt.

Exodus 19:5- 6, *Now therefore, if ye will obey my voice indeed, and keep my covenant, then ye shall be a peculiar treasure unto me above all people: for all the earth is mine: And ye shall be unto me a kingdom of priests, and an holy nation. These are the words which thou shalt speak unto the children of Israel.* (KJV) The children of Abraham and all of those who joined with them are supposed to look differently, eat differently, act differently and worship differently to be an example to the rest of the world. This nation of priests is intended to be the representatives of יהוה on earth.

Notice in the Exodus 19:6 verse that it reads they are *set apart*, the verse does not read they would be righteous. The reasoning being is that being holy does not make one righteous.

BEING HOLY IS A COMMANDMENT
BEING RIGHTEOUS IS
AN OBLIGATION

When the mixed multitude left Egypt they were not a righteous people. They complained, they whined and they begged… a lot. They were prideful and stubborn and it cost them almost everything. They were far from righteous.

Moses defines righteousness in Deuteronomy 6:25, ***And it shall be our righteousness, if we observe to do all these commandments before the Lord our God, as he hath commanded us***. (KJV) Believers are obligated to be obedient as a condition of representing יהוה. Being rebellious or attempting to circumvent the instructions we were given by יהוה negates the covenant to which was agreed and confirmed.

Here would be a good place to put to rest the idea that no one is capable of obeying the covenant. Deuteronomy 30:11–14, ***For this commandment which I command thee this day, it is not hidden from thee, neither is it far off. It is not in heaven, that thou shouldest say, Who shall go up for us to heaven, and bring it unto us, that we may hear it, and do it? Neither is it beyond the sea, that thou shouldest say, Who shall go over the sea for us, and bring it unto us, that we may hear it, and do it? But the word is very nigh unto thee, in thy mouth, and in thy heart, that thou mayest do it.*** (KJV) The instructions are not out of reach and neither can any one claim ignorance of them.

1 John 5:2–3, ***By this we know that we love the children of God, when we love God, and keep his commandments. For this is the love of God, that we keep his commandments: and his commandments are not grievous.*** (KJV) To love is to follow the instructions and they are easy to follow, according to John. Earlier in this epistle John defines sin, 1 John 3:4, ***Whosoever committeth sin transgresseth also the law: for sin is the transgression of the law.*** (KJV)

Twice ישוע told two very different people to go a sin no more The woman caught in adultery is in itself an interesting lesson. (John 8:3–11) According to the covenant both who are caught in adultery must be judged but only the woman is brought. ישוע was not able to accuse her because one can not commit adultery by oneself. The other instance is found in John 5:1–15, ישוע heals a man who had been crippled for thirty eight years. He meets him again a short time later and tells him this in verse 14, ***Afterward Jesus findeth him in the temple, and said unto him, Behold, thou art made whole: sin no more, lest a worse thing come unto thee.*** (KJV) what could possibly be worse than being crippled for thirty eight years? But that is not the most surprising part of this lesson. ישוע tells two people that it is possible not to sin! It is possible to be righteous.

The funny thing about being righteous is that there are a few people in the Bible who are described as being righteous. Zacharias and his wife Elisabeth in Luke 1, Simeon in luke 2. Joseph in Matthew 1, even Cornelius in Acts 10 is considered righteous before he had met Peter. There are others as well and a study of these people will offer insight into what righteousness looks like. Solomon does have this to write about the righteous in Ecclesiastes 7:20, ***Surely there is not a righteous man upon earth, that doeth good, and sinneth not.*** (ASV) How is it possible for one to be considered righteous but still sin? Because we are human. Amos 5:14, ***Seek good, and not evil, that ye may live: and so the LORD, the God of hosts, shall be with you, as ye have spoken.*** (KJV) Yes, humans will make mistakes, our responsibility is to try to be the best we are able to be and not use being human as an excuse because an excuse is inly a reason for failure.

Being righteous doesn't make us perfect, Moses didn't get to walk into the promise land and he had spoken directly to יהוה, if anyone should have crossed the Jordan river it should have been Moses. Being holy doesn't make us righteous, Being holy makes us different. The blood of a lamb doesn't make us righteous, the blood of a lamb allows us the freedom to seek righteousness if one is willing to take the journey.

When one tries to live the way יהוה designed us to live they are seeking righteousness. Following His instructions offers every opportunity to experience each and every aspect of all the word for righteous means. The word translated as righteous is צדיק (tzedeck) and as with many words depending on the context of the sentence it may be translated several different ways. Blameless, innocent, guiltless and right is a short list of what this word may imply. There is a similar word that is typically translated as kindness or charity. חסד (chĕssĕd) this is also translated as mercy, goodness and lovingkindness.

There are many people who practice a type of charity without being righteous. They may give money to the poor or donate it's for a good cause but they do with expecting something in return. Some desire a tax credit, others may look for advertising for their business, some give to boast about how wonderful they are themselves. This is not what real charity is. Real charity requires giving without expecting anything in return. Real charity is helping anonymously. Real charity is offered with love. Real charity will be repaid in blessings being poured out until they are overflowing.

Mercy, is revenge or punishment withheld, even though we deserve whatever vengeance is due. When we choose to overlook an offense, that is mercy. When we choose to forgive, we offer to help carry the burden of the offense. Mercy is not forgiveness, mercy is much like saying, *We will never speak of this again*. The offense remains but the offended party chooses to overlook the offense in favor of hopefully having the opportunity to forgive the offender in the future.

Forgiveness is slightly different in that the one who was offended agrees to help carry the burden of the offense by the offending party. If that sounds complicated, it isn't. Think of it this way, one spouse commits adultery, the other is offended. The burden of the adultery is with the offending spouse, but if the offended or other spouse chooses to forgive the act of adultery, that spouse agrees to help carry the burden. This is far more than the mercy of not getting even, forgiveness is better described as *we will get through this together.*

Mercy and forgiveness should not be confused with grace. Grace is among the most misunderstood Biblical concepts in the modern world. Grace has been promoted and used as a license to sin, a direct conflict with Jude 1:4, **Some people have secretly entered your group. They have already been judged guilty for the things they are doing. Long ago the prophets wrote about these people. They are against God. They have used the grace of our God in the wrong way—to do sinful things.** (ICB)

> *There is far more grace in obedience than will*
> *ever be found in sin*

Grace is what gives us the strength to seek a righteous lifestyle in a fallen world. Grace is far form being a New Testament concept, first found in Genesis 6:8, **But Noah found grace in the eyes of the Lord.** (KJV) Often translated as favor, grace can be found throughout the Old Testament. Grace is so important that it is used to give power to those who may appear powerless.

Deuteronomy 24:1, **When a man hath taken a wife, and married her, and it come to pass that she find no favour in his eyes, because he hath found some unclean-**

ness in her: then let him write her a bill of divorcement, and give it in her hand, and send her out of his house. (KJV) A woman can not request a divorce under the covenant, but if her husband is not living according to the covenant and providing a proper lifestyle for the family it is the responsibility of the woman to remove grace (favor) from the home (no grace in his eyes) until he repents or offers her a divorce. A bill of divorce is required to be a complete document that describes in specific detail why the divorce is necessary so the possible next husband can read it and decide for himself what caused the divorce. The woman seems to be powerless, when indeed she actually held all of the power in the home. That is what grace can do.

Grace is also spiritual sugar, the cells in the human body will always accept a sugar compound as free energy. Grace is exactly that for the spirit as well. When we are feeling low in spirit, grace is the boost we need. Using the marriage analogy again, marriage is not a 50/50 relationship. Each spouse must bring 100%, their complete self to make the relationship 100%. This is *God math*, יהוה Himself will add His 100% because He will never offer less than His best and the relationship is still 100%. When one spouse is having a difficult time, whatever the reason is and they can not offer their 100% that day, יהוה will give what is needed, but not to the spouse who needs it. יהוה will give what is needed to the other spouse to offer that to the one who needs to receive that spiritual sugar. When this happens the relationship remains at 100%, even though יהוה has put in what is necessary to maintain all three are equal at 100%. That how *God math* works. 3 X 100% = 100% complete relationship. Without the grace of יהוה to make up the difference, the relationship can not sustain the stress of being even 1% less than perfect. When we are living the way that

יהוה designed us to live, He will make up the difference for what we may be lacking using His abundance of grace.

Righteousness, mercy, forgiveness and grace are independent of each other and yet they are also interdependent with each other. It is impossible to achieve righteousness without displaying mercy and forgiveness but a righteous person is not made unrighteous because they show mercy without forgiveness. Equally so an unrighteous person can not be made righteous only by forgiving someone without accepting their share of the burden to carry.

The question of how is a person capable of being righteous without forgiving should be addressed. Matthew 6:12, ***And forgive us our debts, as we forgive our debtors.*** (KJV) Is it possible for יהוה not to forgive? Yes, that is why mercy is such an important concept to understand. Ezekiel 18:21–22, ***But if the wicked will turn from all his sins that he hath committed, and keep all my statutes, and do that which is lawful and right, he shall surely live, he shall not die. All his transgressions that he hath committed, they shall not be mentioned unto him: in his righteousness that he hath done he shall live.*** (KJV) According to Ezekiel this is the sacred word of יהוה. There is nothing in this passage that speaks of forgiveness, it does imply that the one who repents is shown mercy because none of their sins will be mentioned. יהוה chooses which burdens He is willing to share with us and some of those burdens are ours to bear alone.

Also notice in this passage that a wicked person is the being spoken of. Prior to repentance they are considered an evildoer. Once the wicked repents and begins to do what is right in the eyes of יהוה then they can be forgiven for any transgressions post repentance but for everything before that point they bear the burden, those transgressions will never be mentioned again by יהוה. After the repentance the once wicked is then offered the opportunity to hear the voice of יהוה and obey His instructions making them one of His people and יהוה their אלהים. Now they are on a place where they can be forgiven.

So how then are we to apply this to our lives since we are made in the image of יהוה? If someone who does not know the person they have offended wrongs them in some way, the offended person can choose to forgive them and share the burden or they may choose not to forgive and never mention the offense again. On the other hand, if it is someone that is familiar, forgiveness is always the better choice because sharing the burden offers the opportunity build the relationship. What spouse who has caught the other in an adulterous situation would never mention that offense again? Probably very few, but many people would be able to live contently knowing that someone they are not familiar with offended them without ever speaking of the offense.

The wicked evildoer who refuses to repent and continues to do evil things has blotted their name from the book of life. No one else will be able to pray and have that name made legible again, the only person who can do that is for the wicked to repent and stop living an evil lifestyle. Failure to repent will result in all of the evil things they have done being used as accusations against them and they will die. Worse for the believers who had repented and rejected the instructions as we see in Ezekiel 18:24, ***But when the righteous turneth away from his righteousness, and committeth iniquity, and doeth according to all the abominations that the wicked man doeth, shall he live? All his righteousness that he hath done shall not be mentioned: in his trespass that he hath trespassed, and in his***

sin that he hath sinned, in them shall he die. (KJV) Keep in mind, this passage from Ezekiel is speaking of the second death mentioned in Revelation 20 and also alluded to in Isaiah 65:17, ***For, behold, I create new heavens and a new earth: and the former shall not be remembered, nor come into mind.*** (KJV) Nothing that was made imperfect by sin will be mentioned after the destruction of the current heaven and earth.

Seeking to walk after יהוה and live in His presence should be the desire for all believers. To achieve that, we are required to prove ourselves worthy in this present life. Because of Adam's rebellion mankind is no longer able to achieve this goal without the mercy and grace of יהוה. His mercy withholds the punishment we deserve while His grace offers us the energy to support our spirit. No one can trick יהוה, His intimate knowledge of our heart reveals to Him those who claim to be repentant but return to a lifestyle of sin and evil. When we deliberately return to sin, we blot our name out of the book of life. Revelation 20:15, ***And whosoever was not found written in the book of life was cast into the lake of fire.*** (KJV)

Most Christian doctrine instructs that simply acknowledging and confessing ones sin along with accepting Jesus into your heart guarantees the visa for heaven is stamped on your passport and you are free to return to your sinful lifestyle without guilt or worry. What this doctrine is selling could be considered *fire insurance* because along with this come the obligation of tithing to the church. Nowhere in the Bible is a believer given permission to return to a sinful lifestyle with the expectation of eternal life. יהוה instructs us that we must hear His voice and obey His commands, not the voice of a religious leader and especially not the conflicting doctrines of any religious system.

Many churches claim their doctrine is *based* on the Bible. So what! The doctrine of the Satanic Temple is based on the Bible also, without the Bible there is no השטן, (ha-satahn) the adversary, Satan. Instead of basing your doctrine on the Bible, try a radical approach, make the sacred word of יהוה your doctrine. There are churches that will teach things contrary to the Bible and cause people to become disillusioned with יהוה because these trusting souls are net witnessing miracles, healings or anything else that they expected. The reason they are not able to witness these things is because they have believed the lies that our fathers passed on to us. Just say this prayer and you will go to heaven, if we ask in the name of Jesus we can get anything we want. The contradictions belong to mankind. God wants you to have everything you want in life, you can be rich if you just proclaim it. That doesn't conform to Matthew 19:24, ***And again I say unto you, It is easier for a camel to go through the eye of a needle, than for a rich man to enter into the kingdom of God*** (KJV)

That doesn't mean that a wealthy person can't enter the kingdom, Abraham and Job were very wealthy but so was the rich man described in Luke 16. Financial status has nothing to do with eternal life, that comes from the heart and to whom you choose to listen. Abraham and job were wealthy because they chose to be obedient and their obedience brought the blessings that allowed them to become rich. A selfish prayer begging for a full bank account will not be heard.

God math, makes even someone with no money rich when they receive the blessing יהוה pours out on them. We receive those blessings when we do what is right in the eyes of יהוה. That is the path to righteousness and it opens the door to mercy, grace and forgiveness. Rejecting the lies we have inherited and embracing the sacred word of יהוה, then living the way He designed us to live is the way to experience Luke 6:38, ***Give, and it will be given to you. A good measure, pressed down, shaken together, and running over will be poured into your lap. For with the measure you use, it will be measured back to you.*** (BSB) This isn't speaking of putting money in the offering, this is about how we really are treating our neighbor. Being merciful, graceful and even sharing someones burden brings the blessings our spirit desires from יהוה and fulfills our obligation to righteousness.

AVOID THE BRIMSTONE

When I wrote *Tradition To Truth, One Man's Search For Honest Answers*[5] I write of the importance of the Biblical feasts. I was missing one critical piece of information at that time but through further study and revelation was able to discover the difference between redemption and atonement the way that the writers of the New Testament would understand. Redemption is a repurchase of something or the repurchase of slave or prisoner. Atonement is more of a reconciliation after an unpleasant argument. This understanding perfectly explains why the Blood of ישוע at Passover is used to repurchase humankind from the enemy after two major events. First being Adam eating the fruit and allowing sin to enter the world making what was perfect, now imperfect and the other is the violation of the covenant at Mount Sinai with the golden calf. The blood of ישוע is buys us back, if we choose to return to יהוה, that blood can not reconcile us with יהוה and to try and force that concept destroys the shadow picture of Yom Kippur.

---

[5]   Tradition To Truth, One Man's Search For Honest Answers Lulu Publishing Services, 2017.

Exodus 17:3, ***Behold, I will stand before you there on the rock at Horeb, and you shall strike the rock, and water shall come out of it, and the people will drink." And Moses did so, in the sight of the elders of Israel.*** (ESV) When Moses strikes the rock and life giving water flowed from it, he was instructed to strike the rock. Moses was well on his way to being a prophet's prophet, listening to יהוה and speaking what he had been instructed to speak and doing what he was instructed to do. Forty years later, Moses receives a different instruction, Numbers 20:8, ***Take the rod, and gather thou the assembly together, thou, and Aaron thy brother, and speak ye unto the rock before their eyes; and it shall give forth his water, and thou shalt bring forth to them water out of the rock: so thou shalt give the congregation and their beasts drink.*** (KJV) This is a different rock and after forty years of hearing the people complain, Moses was irritable. The people had seen all of the things that יהוה had done for them, they witnessed all of the wonders and heard Him speak but their pride prevented them from trusting the way that Moses was able to trust. For the first time, Moses disobeys יהוה and he will regret it. Numbers 20:10-11, ***And Moses and Aaron gathered the congregation together before the rock, and he said unto them, Hear now, ye rebels; must we fetch you water out of this rock? And Moses lifted up his hand, and with his rod he smote the rock twice: and the water came out abundantly, and the congregation drank, and their beasts also.*** (KJV) Because Moses is disobedient in his anger and strikes the rock instead of speaking to the rock, he destroys a shadow picture of ישוע. This deliberate sin prevents Moses from entering the promise land, He will be able to view it from where his life ends but he would never enter it. We will never know what could have been if Moses had followed the instruction to speak to the rock.

The Feasts are rehearsals for good things to come, Along with the feasts we have examples of the way people lived and the result of their action. Solomon writes in his introduction to Ecclesiastes, *There is nothing new under the sun.* Earlier you read, a good litmus test to verify what is in the New Testament is to find a witness for it in the Old Testament and this works well for the things we do also. Deuteronomy 12:30, **take care that you be not ensnared to follow them, after they have been destroyed before you, and that you do not inquire about their gods, saying, 'How did these nations serve their gods?—that I also may do the same.** ESV) We are not to worship יהוה the way other people worship their אלהים. יהוה considers it to be disgustingly detestable to worship Him using the same manner of worship used for anything else.

Because יהוה requires us to worship Him following His instructions, the question becomes how should we speak to Him? There are many example in the Bible of how we are to speak to יהוה. Something to remember is John 4:24, **God is a Spirit: and they that worship Him must worship Him in spirit and in truth.** (KJV) Because יהוה is spirit, we must actually speak to Him with spirit. This means our prayers need to be spoken to allow our spirit to reach His hears.

In 1 Samuel we are introduced to Hannah, a woman described as barren. When she went to Shilo for a feast Hannah was mocked for not having children. After a meal when others had been drinking heavily, Hannah went to the temple where the priests were to pray. 1 Samuel 1:13, **Now Hannah, she spake in her heart; only her lips moved, but her voice was not reheard: therefore Eli thought she had been drunken.** (KJV) Because Eli did not hear her speak he thought she was drunk as well, upon finding out she was not drunk but praying he immediately interceded on her behalf, audibly asking יהוה to grant what is in Hannah's heart.

Daniel was so willing to have יהוה hear his prayer that he risked his life. When Darius was king, the law was passed that no one could pray to anyone except the king. Daniel had a choice to make, he could have kept quiet, he could have simply offered a silent prayer but Daniel knew he needed to release his spirit so that it could connect with the spirit of יהוה. Daniel went do far as to open a window so His spirit would not be detained in any way. Daniel 8:10, ***Now when Daniel knew that the writing was signed, he went into his house; and his windows being open in his chamber toward Jerusalem, he kneeled upon his knees three times a day, and prayed, and gave thanks before his God, as he did aforetime.*** (KJV) The King's men overheard Daniel praying to יהוה and reported it to the king. This is the reason Daniel spent the night with the lions.

Yes, יהוה knows what is in our heart and what is on our mind, that doesn't mean that our spirit has actually been released to him as we exhale and speak. (Spirit is discussed in an earlier chapter) ישוע gives some advice on prayer, Matthew 6:7, ***When you pray, don't babble like the idolaters, since they imagine they'll be heard for their many words.*** (HCSB) Quite literally don't use empty, meaningless repetitive phrases. This warning is issued to contrast the way the pagans pray to their idols who are not even gods. Elijah has some fun with the pagans on Mount Carmel with the four hundred-fifty prophets of Baal. 1 Kings 18:26–27, ***And they took the bullock which was given them, and they dressed it, and called on the name of Baal from morning even until noon, saying, O Baal, hear us. But there was no voice, nor any that answered.***

And they leaped upon the altar which was made. And it came to pass at noon, that Elijah mocked them, and said, Cry aloud: for he is a god; either he is talking, or he is pursuing, or he is in a journey, or peradventure he sleepeth, and must be awaked. (KJV) The prophets cried out all morning repeating the same useless words begging for some response until Elijah began to tease them. Then the prophets began to cut themselves hoping for a response but none came, Baal was silent, they had been praying to an אלהים who was not יהוה אלהים and no amount of obnoxious babbling would entice Baal to answer.

Glossolalia is the term for speaking in tongues. Many believe this is a phenomenon that originated in Acts chapter 2 when the Holy Spirit gave the disciples a *gift* to speak in tongues. These same people would be saddened to know that the act of speaking in tongues was a pagan practice well before the 1st century AD. As mentioned in an earlier chapter, what happened in Acts 2 was most likely not tongues but people being so overwhelmed they spoke in the language they were most familiar with. Glossolalia, however is speaking in a language completely unknown and there are very few documented occurrences of this actually happening in a Christian church setting and even those are suspicious. Glossolalia, is believed to have first been practiced by the ancient Samaritans around the 10th century BC. The utter gibberish that was spoken by the priest and prophets was intended to make the general population believe they were speaking the language of the אלהים. Glossolalia was also practiced in ancient China and among the Eskimo Shaman.

Paul writes to the Corinthians about glossolalia in 1 Corinthians 14, and advises them not to use this unwisely. 1 Corinthians 14:19–20, *I thank God that I speak in other languages more than all of you; yet in the church I would rather speak five words with my understanding, in order to teach others also, than 10,000 words in another language*. (HCSB) Paul isn't writing that he uses glossolalia, but that he speaks many different languages and uses them to teach other about the glory of יהוה.

The Protestant reformation also revived glossolalia in theChristian church. Even John Wesley who founded the Methodist movement and his brother Charles Wesley who wrote many Hymns are believed to have practiced glossolalia. Joseph Smith who founded the Latter Day Saints movement advised those of the Mormon faith to stand when they practiced glossolalia. There are Christian denominations founded on the practice of glossolalia, some go so far as to teach that one who does not speak in tongues does not have the Holy Spirit.

Some try to use Acts 10:46, *For they heard them speak with tongues, and magnify God. Then answered Peter*, (KJV) as proof glossolalia is a gift of the Holy Spirit. The problem is this verse simply reads that the Jewish men who were present heard the family of Cornelius speaking in a different language to praise יהוה, a language which they obviously understood. If this had been nothing more than uttering gibberish no one would have been able to say what was being said without interpretation and none is mentioned in this passage.

During the 19th and 20th centuries studies were conducted by doctors and by theologians attempting to verify or discredit glossolalia as a genuine religious practice. What was discovered is nothing less than surprising. Practically all who studied the phenomenon are convinced it is nothing more than a charade, few believe that glossolalia is a language of spirits (plural) including demons. Only a few of the Christian theologians indicate they are convinced it is a gift of the Holy Spirit. יהוה instructs us not to worship Him the way other peoples worship their idols and that obviously includes using glossolalia. One would have a very strong argument that the practice of glossolalia to worship or pray to יהוה would be something that He would find at least offensive and probably consider it an abomination. Deuteronomy 12:30–32, ***They will be destroyed for you. Be careful not to be trapped by asking about their gods. Don't say, "How do these nations worship? I will do the same." Don't worship the Lord your God that way. The Lord hates the evil ways they worship their gods. They even burn their sons and daughters as sacrifices to their gods! Be sure to do everything I have commanded you. Do not add anything to it. And do not take anything away from it***. (ICB) Prayer is a form of communication and it is also a form of worship. The lies we have inherited are many and they have found a way into every aspect of our relationship with יהוה.

Prayer is the most important weapon we have in our battle with evil. Prayer allows mankind an interaction with יהוה, who is the most powerful force known in heaven or on earth. He demands and deserves the most respect we have to offer and yet He also desires us to include Him when we celebrate, when we laugh, when we cry and when we grieve. People often think they have no idea how to pray, one place to begin is with the words of David in Psalm 139:23, ***Search me, O God, and know my heart: try me, and know my thoughts***: (KJV) Giving יהוה permission to search out your inner most concerns and troubles and allowing Him to resolve any issues His way can be a good place to begin.

When we reach out to the power of יהוה, we should expect great things. Of course we must remember that to communicate with Him we must be willing to humble ourselves and expect that whatever happens will happen the way He desires it, not the way we may think it should happen. We must also be willing to live the way He designed us to live, Isaiah 1:15, ***And when ye spread forth your hands, I will hide mine eyes from you: yea, when ye make many prayers, I will not hear: your hands are full of blood.*** (KJV) If we have not been (or trying to be) obedient, He will refuse to even hear us. Only when we are attempting to live HIs way will יהוה offer us His mercy and her us.

When we are speaking to יהוה we should be careful with what we say. While we don't need to worry about sounding perfect in any language, our heart should agree with our mind when we speak. If we are confused and don't know what to say, that is no excuse not to pray, on the contrary, that is exactly when we need to pray. Express that you don't know what to say, יהוה will understand better than you do. Give Him permission to figure out what is best for you instead of trying to dictate control over יהוה. Prayer should not be reduced to a list of demands:

Dear God,
Please heal Mr. So-and-so from their disease.
Please help the children.
Please do this, Please do that.
Amen, oh and thank you,

Prayer can be powerful, prayer can be invigorating and prayer can be intimidating. Ask a group of people, *Who like to lead us in prayer?* Chances are there will be nervous looks until someone finally speaks up and accepts the blessing. When ישוע was asked by his disciples to teach them to pray he gave us the example known as the *Lord's Prayer*, this comes from the concepts outlined in the Old Testament.

Because having many children is considered to be a blessing, ישוע blesses יהוה by addressing Him as our Father. Next he honors יהוה by considering Him set apart and Holy. Allowing יהוה to be our אלהים and having complete control over us and the world is may Your will be accomplished not what we may want. Allow us what we need to live, when we make a mistake forgive us and allow us to forgive others and keep us from being tested because we may fail. ישוע ends with protect us from evil. This model of prayer has been used for centuries and remains an exceptional guide for our personal prayer life. Don't worry about sounding *churchy* or using the right words, יהוה is far more concerned with the honesty of what you are saying, not the vocabulary you use however you should try to use words that you actually understand.

When we allow our doctrines and traditions to guide the way we worship יהוה we will miss the blessings He desires for us to have. A famine from blessings can be much worse than starvation. Failing to receive the blessing from יהוה robs us of having the productive, successful, joyous and abundant life He want us to enjoy. Accepting the lies we have inherited as truth actually has the potential of preventing us from entering into eternal life. When we are not receiving the blessings we can become depressed and disillusioned with יהוה. This leads to rejecting Him and ignoring His involvement in our life. We may go so far as to blot our name from the book keeping us from eternal life and securing our place in the lake of fire.

There is good news, you can avoid the lake of steaming hot brimstone, all you need to do is reject the traditions and doctrines of man and listen for the voice of יהוה and then do as He asks, follow HIs instructions.

THE TORAH SYNDROME

Let's get personal, I have probably made many people uncomfortable with the things I have written and I do not apologize for that. If you have been treating traditions or man made doctrines with equal or more respect than the sacred word of יהוה, you need to be uncomfortable. No one person or one religion has a monopoly on getting everything 100% right or wrong. Having written that, it is time to examine the reasons people are leaving the mainstream religions and this is where things can get complicated.

The mainstream media seems to hate religion, any religion unless everyone is bowing down to them. Watching every show and reading every article they write. Some have stopped reporting the news and are influencing the news. Now many in the media are trying to tell you how you should live your life. Sadly most people don't realize that many of the so called news shows are only opinion shows that need to sell advertising to remain on the air. Many politicians around the world appear on these opinion talk shows to promote their agenda or the agenda of their particular party while degrading their opponent. The one thing that all of these people have in common is they hate anything that distracts the viewer, reader or listener.

With much of the population turned into media zombies, the rest of the world is forced to either capitulate and risk being drawn into the chaos or simply step into the background. With many churches being transformed into little more than social clubs through their progressive doctrines and other major denominations dividing themselves, the mainstream Christian religion seems to be in disarray. Or that is what the media would have you believe.

There are quite a lot of people walking out of their denominations, what is not being reported is where they are going. Most of the exodus from the Christian churches are from people feeling discouraged by the increasingly widening divide between church doctrine and the Bible. Most of the people I speak with about leaving their church didn't want to leave. They love the people and they enjoy the music and many things about their worship community. The main reason most people leave is because they realize what they are reading in the Bible is not the same message that comes from the pulpit.

Pastors hate to lose congregants, especially the ones who fill up the offering. When a large donor happens to mention their view on a subject, that view has a way of becoming the view of the whole church, even if it conflicts with the sacred word of יהוה. When this happens, the people who choose to stand on Biblical authority are often the ones to leave the church. Once finances are allowed the power of influence, Biblical interpretation becomes contaminated. Mathew 6:24, ***No one can serve two masters, for either he will hate the one and love the other, or he will be devoted to the one and despise the other. You cannot serve God and money.*** (ESV)

Ideally, an organized group of people who have plenty of money to achieve their goals should be able to do so without strife, but this is not an ideal world. Too often complacency replaces resilience and the people begin to realize they are not of one accord and grace does not abound. The common goal is no longer recognized by the whole and the resulting division creates conflict. This same principle is not limited to churches, it applies to families and civic organizations as well. Often the one thing that bonds these groups of people together is having a common enemy. That enemy may be anything from poverty and hunger to a desire for something or a seemingly impossible goal. Poor families tend to depend on each other until they *strike it rich* and lust and greed begin to encroach. Churches often have a goal of reaching into the community to help in some way or maybe they want to build a new building. While the task of raising funds is daunting, when that is what binds the church together instead of their love for יהוה, there will be a division after the goal is achieved.

Any church or group of people will have issues, there will always be those who think their way is the best way to accomplish whatever goal the group chooses to accomplish. In Acts chapter 1 we see the disciples trying to replace Judas and failing miserably because they were trying to force their ideas into a plan that יהוה was already working on. A family or civic organization has an advantage over a church in one very important aspect, the church is expected to follow Biblical principle and authority. A family who suddenly has no financial worries is almost expected to divide. The Civic organization has only their own bylaws to guide their action but the church or other group of believers who claim to believe the Bible are seen as hypocritical when they stray from the accepted normal operating procedures for a religious organization.

Face the facts, when a church or similar group fails to uphold Biblical authority they are hypocritical. Condoning anything that the Bible forbids as sin is failing to conform to the Biblical principles they claim to represent. Enter the faithful few, the people who actually believe and read the Bible. These are the people that some in the churches and Synagogues consider to be radical. These are the people who are so demanding, they demand accountability from the leaders who follow their man made regulations instead of Biblical authority and principle. These people are so arrogant as to demand that people who represent יהוה actually follow His instructions. These are often the pastor's worst nightmare because they actually study the Bible more in-depth than most seminaries teach. These are not the average seat warmers who are simply attending a religious service because it seems like the right thing to do.

What changes someone from average attendee into a zealot? For some it is a need to know the truth, for others it is a desire for that close relationship with the אלהים they have been hearing about but can't seem to achieve. There are certainly other reasons that drive people to search for answers, some may realize that the traditions leave them feeling empty and others who may say their spirit simply was never satisfied. For what ever reason these people begin to dig into the Bible, to study in various ways that bring them peace and then sometimes something happens that causes these people sleepless nights. A piece of the puzzle has been revealed to them, they begin searching for people with pieces that may match theirs and through divine appointments they begin to find the other pieces. For some simply giving someone else their piece was their message and for others, they are driven even deeper into the sacred word of יהוה.

Most of the people described this way have no interest in becoming a pastor, preacher or priest. These are the people who are ordained not by mankind but by יהוה himself. John 15:16, ***Ye have not chosen me, but I have chosen you, and ordained you, that ye should go and bring forth fruit, and that your fruit should remain: that whatsoever ye shall ask of the Father in my name, he may give it you.*** (KJV) When יהוה chooses someone for whatever purpose, the knowledge of that appointment may not always reflect 1 Samuel 3:10, ***And the LORD came, and stood, and called as at other times, Samuel, Samuel. Then Samuel answered, Speak; for thy servant heareth.*** (KJV) Not every person receives such a direct approach. For some, it may be another suggesting they have a special talent for delivering a message יהוה wants them to deliver. For others it may be an old lady near death who mistakes you for the *Parson.* These divine ordinations are far more valuable than any that man could bestow on man. With these divine ordinations we have provision provided by יהוה to accomplish the task.

Not everyone is assigned the task of teacher or leader, some of the most important tasks are that of support. When we think of a mentor today, we often get the image in our mind of someone who teaches and leads a younger person into adulthood. The actual role of mentor is not to lead someone down a certain path, it is to help the younger person find the path that יהוה strongly desires they follow. A mentor is not a master craftsman instructing an apprentice, A mentor should be the greatest support system the young person has. A great mentor will help the young person realize that doing the right thing is easy and doing the wrong thing is difficult. Sometimes when people find themselves in a position of divine appointment they don't realize their role is to help others find their place in the Kingdom of יהוה and not to rule with their own authority.

Christians seem especially overwhelmed when they realize they have been ordained by יהוה for some purpose. They begin to understand that the traditions and denominational doctrines are nothing more than the empty lies we have inherited and become confused and disoriented in the way they apply their faith to their life. This doesn't mean they lose their faith, trust or love for יהוה or ישוע, it means the way they practice and walk out that faith becomes less motivated by tradition and all of their energy is directed in following the sacred word of יהוה. Some have described this as recognizing the lies we have inherited from our fathers, others have said their spirit suddenly felt alive again. But this doesn't mean that they have reached the end of their journey, for many their persecution is just beginning.

When a person finally understands the difference between the sacred word of יהוה and the lies of tradition and man made doctrine they can never return to the world of ignorance, no matter how well intentioned they may be. Many describe listening to modern religious leaders as wolves in sheep's clothing regardless of the denomination and often regardless of religion. Some try to remain silent while attempting to lead a life that is led by Biblical principle but find that is impossible because the word of יהוה will not be silent. Some try to share what they have discovered in the Bible and their excitement is met with a barrage of negative comments. What is so sad is that the people who refuse to accept the Bible are supposed to be representing the Bible to the world.

Everyone reaches a point when they must choose, leave what is familiar and venture out into the unknown or knowingly and willingly reject something too majestic and full of awe and wonder to be dismissed. Often Christians who find themselves in this situation must prepare themselves to run through the gauntlet of criticism and failed narratives. Some may try to move from church to church or even denomination to denomination but are never satisfied. Quite often the Christian will think *Hey, Jesus was a jew, maybe I should find out what that's all about.* They begin to investigate modern day Judaism as if that was the religion during the 1st century. A few may even go to a synagogue and speak to a Rabbi and while that is definitely beneficial from a Bible study aspect, even the Rabbi's would say that Judaism today isn't practiced the way it was twenty centuries ago.

Eventually these Christian, pilgrims will find the Torah, the books of Moses, the first five books of the Old Testament. What happens next has been aptly named by a dear friend as; the *Torah syndrome.* In their excitement to be obedient to יהוה, they read about or listen to everything they can to learn as much as they can as fast as they can. They learn about the 613 commandments and how we must follow each and every one, until they understand that some of those are only for men, some only for women, some for children and others just for animals. Of the 613 the instructions for the Livitical priesthood make up the most which means that unless you are a priest in the Temple you have far less than 613 commandments to follow.

The most valuable lessons someone new to Torah can learn are about the Feasts of יהוה. These feasts describe His appointed times, when He chooses to meet with us and when He desires special attention. Learning to worship

יהוה the way He chooses for us to worship Him not only strengthens our relationship to Him, it also denies us the opportunity to worship other אלהים (gods with the small g). While it is easy to fall into the trap of following the traditions associated with the feasts, these traditions are quickly identified and resolved. After all recently learned traditions are much easier to quit than the traditions and doctrines that have been embedded in our mind.

Another problem the Torah baby (another term from a different friend) must face is that of the calendar. Currently there are about twelve different calendars to choose from for following the feast days. Again, a good rule of thumb is to find what is written in the Old Testament, search it out in Hebrew without needing to resort to any references mentioned on another language. When someone needs to reference material from a source other than the Bible, be very careful. There are charlatans who are more than willing to take your money and waste your time. There are tremendous reputable resources available and most are free.

The commandments, the feasts, and the calendar are just a few things that the enemy will use to trap you in your quest to know יהוה. Living a Biblical lifestyle doesn't look like you're dressing in robes and rags. Living a Biblical lifestyle doesn't mean all you can eat is locusts and wild honey either. Eating Biblically (according to the instructions in Leviticus 11) is a very healthy diet. I need to make a personal observation at this point; *I am amazed at how many Christians degrade someone when they choose to live according to the Bible.* Yes, I have personally experienced the harsh words from family and friends when I choose not to eat pork or lobster. There is nothing in the original manuscripts of the Bible to indicate the dietary laws have been rescinded, ישוע is recorded as saying he did not come to change the law (Matthew 5:17, ***Think not that I am come to destroy the law, or the prophets: I am not come to destroy, but to fulfil.*** (KJV)) and he never ate anything that would have violated the covenant or he would not have been able to pay the price of redemption. Anything that would suggest the dietary laws have been altered or done away with is one more of the lies we have inherited from our fathers. No one is able to live a set apart or Holy life when they are not actually set apart.

Because the people seeking truth rather than tradition become discouraged anyone who actually finds their way to walk with יהוה deserves that honor. Within every Christian denomination including the Messianic/ Hebrew Roots community there is an element that desires to appear to look like every other *normal* church or synagogue. Some go so far as to include the entertainment factor as part of their regular worship. Don't think that I'm eluding to anything here that I am not. There is a time for the entertainment before and or after the main focal point of worship which should be centered on יהוה. Nothing should interfere with His time to be worshipped. Prior to that time beginning there should be a time of celebration, after His set apart time social interaction, entertainment or a time to enjoy each other is necessary. There is however the thought among some Christian and even Messianic fellowships that they stop the weekly service for dancing and song. The purpose for this is to prevent people from coming only for the entertainment or the food without hearing the message. This will be a odd statement, I would much rather speak with a few people who have a desire to hear about the great things that יהוה is doing than speak to a large group of people who are sitting through what I have to say as they wait for the dancing and singing to begin.

The illustration we read in the Bible is for each community or neighborhood to have small fellowships that would meet at least once each week. Then three times every year the men were required to make the pilgrimage to gather for Passover, Shavuot and Sukkot. Even though only the men were actually required to make the trip, not many would make these trips without their families. Luke 2:42–45, ***And when he was twelve years old, they went up to Jerusalem after the custom of the feast. And when they had fulfilled the days, as they returned, the child Jesus tarried behind in Jerusalem; and Joseph and his mother knew not of it. But they, supposing him to have been in the company, went a day's journey; and they sought him among their kinsfolk and acquaintance. And when they found him not, they turned back again to Jerusalem, seeking him.*** (KJV) What this describes is a group of people traveling together, so large was the group that a twelve year old wasn't seen for a day and no one was immediately concerned.

The Pilgrimage feasts were annual events, the שבת Shabbat or Sabbath began at sundown on the sixth day and lasted until sundown on the seventh day. The communities would gather together to hear a word from the teachers or other members of the community who had something revealed to them. Colossians 3:16, ***Let the word of Christ dwell in you richly in all wisdom; teaching and admonishing one another in psalms and hymns and spiritual songs, singing with grace in your hearts to the LORD.*** (KJV) Thankfully an increasing number of communities are beginning to return to this example. Small fellowships have people meeting in each other's homes for Bible study or prayer meetings. When these are open to the public a small sign may be seen in front of the home. I am familiar with a few people around the country who make the use of a larger room available for the young people in the community to gather and play music or sing and the only requirement is thirty minutes of uninterrupted Bible study before they leave for the evening. One of these places has the Bible study led by a Christian pastor and a Rabbi.

After the new pilgrim has run the gambit of commands, feasts, calendar, food and feeling alone they finally search for a local fellowship and there are many around. The more well known of the Messianic/Hebrew roots ministries have websites with fellowship finders to connect like minded believers. These can be great resources used properly, do your homework. Hopefully the new pilgrim will survive the *Torah syndrome* and find a fellowship where they can grow their faith and trust in יהוה and be the example to the world they are ordained to be.

One very important item that should be discouraged for the small fellowships, don't think you need to look like a church or a synagogue. There is no reason when you are meeting in each other's homes to outgrow your ordination. In other words, don't try to be like a big church, you don't need a bank account and you don't need to become a 501 C-3 tax exempt corporation. If you began your fellowship to get rich, you will fail. יהוה did not ordain you have money in the bank, He ordained you to deliver a message of some kind to someone else or many other people.

When you are new to a fellowship, remember it's OK if they don't do it like someone else does it. Not everyone has the gift of music or dance but everyone has *a* gift. One question that is asked is if a fellowship should ask a church if they can meet in their building? There is no one size fits all answer for that. If a fellowship needs room for a special event such as a celebration of a feast and a church has a room available, use it. If your fellowship is growing large enough that you can not fit everyone in the place you are meeting, that is a great problem to have. the best suggestion is for the fellowship to consider dividing. That may sound scary, but if the fellowship is growing for the right reasons, the best way is to reproduce what is working. Allowing different families to host the fellowship so that it can continue to develop is a terrific way to ensure the small house fellowship feeling that so many people enjoy remains a vital part of what you have started.

What to do if there is no like minded fellowship in your area? Start one. Chances are you are not the only person in your area who wants to experience a joyous relationship with יהוה. Think about the church you may have been attending, were there people there who didn't think you were completely crazy because you believed what was written in the Bible? This doesn't need to be anything formal, in fact it is better if it isn't. Begin by asking some believing friends if they would be interested in an informal Bible study and open your home for a couple of hours either one/week or by-weekly. This isn't rocket science and your not trying to save the whales, this is Bible study. Reading the selected passages and discussing how they apply to our lives today. Eventually you will be able to introduce the idea that we should live the way יהוה designed us to live. You will have been the example, you will have delivered the message you were ordained to deliver.

The progression of the *Torah Syndrome* often follows this pattern;

- Realization of Biblical truth.
- Searching for answers.
- Dissatisfaction with standard responses of traditions and doctrine.

- Seeking anyone who may have the same feeling.
- Thinking you're crazy.
- Wondering if you're Jewish and examining Jewish traditions.
- Realizing the practice of Jewish traditions don't always follow the Sacred word of יהוה.

Looking at the Messianic/Hebrew Roots movement and finding out they are trying to find the answers too.

After all of this, the new pilgrim will realize that to have the real peace and comfort they are searching for they must give up all of the traditions of man and simply embrace the Sacred word of יהוה. Only after all of the seeking and searching, does one understand that no amount of praise music, no amount of dancing and no amount of following these rules or those rules will ever satisfy your spirit and your soul as much as simply living the way יהוה designed you to live. To be obedient to His word... Just to relax and enjoy the life that is fulfilled by including יהוה in all aspects of your life. The slogan WWJD, *What would Jesus do?* has an answer and all we need to do is read the Bible. When ישוע was challenged by the things of the world, he found the place where it was written in the sacred word of יהוה and he did what was written.

Matthew 4:3, ***And when the tempter came to him, he said, If thou be the Son of God, command that these stones be made bread***. (KJV) When ישוע answered he quoted Deuteronomy 8:3, ***And he humbled thee, and suffered thee to hunger, and fed thee with manna, which thou knewest not, neither did thy fathers know; that he might make thee know that <u>man doth not live by bread only, but by every word that proceedeth out of the mouth of the LORD</u> doth man live***. (KJV) ***Matthew 4:6, And*** *saith unto him, If thou be the Son of God, cast thyself down: for it is written, He shall give his angels charge concerning thee: and in their hands they shall bear thee up, lest at any time thou dash thy foot against a stone.* (KJV) (*The enemy actually twists Psalms 91:12–13*) *And the answer from Isaiah 7:12, But Ahaz said, I will not ask, neither will I tempt the LORD.* (KJV)

Matthew 4:9, *And saith unto him, All these things will I give thee, if thou wilt fall down and worship me.* (KJV) And from Deuteronomy 6:13–14, *Thou shalt fear the Lord thy God, and serve him, and shalt swear by his name. Ye shall not go after other gods, of the gods of the people which are round about you;* (KJV)

ישוע is recorded as using the expression, *It is written,* about thirty times (depending on which translation you read) and some of these accounts are recored from the same events. Even so, it should be evident that ישוע relies on what is written to teach the people around him. He also uses the phrase, *you have heard it said,* when he is making a distinction that divides tradition or doctrine from the sacred word of יהוה. This should be an easily recognizable example for us to follow. There is no need to interpret or *guess* WWJD, we simply need to follow his example.

ישוע didn't allow himself to be trapped by the lies we have inherited. He chose to be obedient, he chose to listen to the voice of יהוה and he chose to do what he was assigned to do. That is the example we have for us to emulate and ultimately that is the destination of those who choose to suffer through the *Torah syndrome*. The journey is worthwhile and the rewards are unimaginably exquisite. If you find yourself on this journey, don't stop and don't look back, *no one who has one hand on the plow and looks back is fit for the kingdom of יהוה*.

THE NEW WORLD ORDER OF

The conspiracy theorists seem to enjoy sharing their views of the New World Order. Put those words in any search engine and the results seem endless. TheNew World Order has prompted a large portion of the worlds population regardless of religion to prepare for whatever scenario one may envision. The problem is that the worst case scenario we prepare for today will change before it has a chance to happen. While so many people are convinced the New World Order will be a political scheme cooked up by the elite of the world to enslave the masses to do their bidding, we can be certain that the result of the coming New World Order will be much, much worse than anyone can currently imagine.

If the New World Order was as simple as the elite rich such as the Bilderberg's or the Free Mason's or even the Catholic Church attempting to take control of the world, there would be nothing to worry about. The masses of people around the world would easily be able to rebel against any such power grab on a global scale using nothing more than the overwhelming population. Even one million elite people can not control 7.9 billion people. They would easily be outnumbered because they would never be able to amass the forces necessary to control the rest of the population.

Realizing that a forced take-over is not a viable option, then there is the political alternative to consider. While politics is one of the vehicles being used to achieve the One World Order, the political arena can not deliver all of the nations of the world into the hands of only a few who want to control the world. Religions have been dividing people all over the world since the plains of Shinar, where the tower of Babel was destroyed. This means that religion can not be a viable option to achieve the One World Order either.

To understand the force necessary to bring a New World Order into existence, one needs to stop searching for the earthly means of delivering the majority of mankind into the hands of the few. Change the question and ask what would be needed to accomplish this travesty? The answer can be found in the sacred words of יהוה. There are passages in the bible that are overlooked by Christians because they have been taught that they have no significant connection to the coming of the reigning messiah. These same passages are not a priority among the Rabbinic scholars because they have been taught that these words are prophecy already fulfilled or for a different purpose. Beginning in Psalm 82:1–2, **God has taken his place in the divine council; in the midst of the gods he holds judgment: "How long will you judge unjustly and show partiality to the wicked?** (ESV) Literally David writes, אלהים *stands in the divine congregation among the* אלהים *and judges.* His use of the title אלהימ removes any friendly or familiar connotation. יהוה is furious, if there were a more harsh word to describe how angry He is feel free to use it. This isn't a poetic divine council, this is a father who has called a family meeting to deliver the most harsh sentence he can impose on his children, in this passage it is death.

Psalm 82:6–7, I said, ***"You are gods, sons of the Most High, all of you; nevertheless, like men you shall die, and fall like any prince."*** (ESV) יהוה has condemned these lesser divine beings, (gods with a small *g*) to death for failing to properly care for mankind. The questions of who these divine beings are, why they were supposed to be looking after mankind and how did all of that happen needs to be addressed. What happened in the garden with the serpent is mankind's first involvement with the rebellious השטן (ha-satahn) the adversary, better known as Satan.

Adam's sin is far more serious than simply eating the forbidden fruit, the perfect world that Adam knew could no longer be perfect. יהוה had given Adam dominion of the world and this is a poor understanding of a fair translation. What was given to Adam is better described as a caretakers authority. As long as Adam was following the instructions he had from יהוה everything remained perfect. When Adam failed to follow those explicit instructions, he was no longer eligible to continue in his position. Adam's authority over the world was removed. There are some denominations who argue that this is when the adversary gained control of the world but it is not. As יהוה was judging Adam and Eve, He refused to allow the adversary to have any authority over a perfect world. He cursed the earth with thorns and briars and other nasty things that would have the ability to harm mankind. The process of dying began for Adam and Eve, they were ejected from the garden and the guard was placed at the entrance to prevent mankind eating from the tree of life. Had Adam been allowed to eat from the tree of life and live forever in this world, he would have condemned all of us to live forever under the rule of the adversary.

By cursing the earth, יהוה is denying the adversary the opportunity to twist perfection for evil purpose. By allowing mankind to die a physical death in this world, יהוה is preparing us for the opportunity to have eternal life in the future. The adversary knows he is in a battle he can not win, his ultimate goal is to prevent יהוה from having a relationship with as many human beings as possible. Don't make the mistake of thinking we are pawns or cannon fodder in this spiritual war. The adversary doesn't think that highly of mankind and יהוה continues to protect those who choose Him in many ways. Noah is one of the ways יהוה has ensured that mankind is eligible to remain on the earth. For evil to be so prevalent that יהוה was questioning Himself about mankind, He still decided we were worth fighting for.

After the flood of Noah, the people were told to spread over the whole earth, instead they chose to gather in one place on the plain of Shinar. In Genesis 10, we read what is known as the *table of nations*, this describes the seventy nations, who they came from and how they would be disbursed around the world. יהוה assigned a divine being over selected geographic areas to watch over these nations as they settled around the world. These are the divine beings we read about in Psalm 82, the same divine beings who were loyal to יהוה as long as the majority of the people in their assigned territory were faithful to יהוה. There was a great amount of grace offered from יהוה as these people went out from the plains of Shinar, after just a couple of generations they really didn't understand how to worship or serve יהוה, the people were trying but couldn't quite get it right but as long as they were trying the divine beings were bound to be loyal to יהוה also.

There was one geographic location that יהוה did not assign to any other divine being, the land that He would promise to Abraham יהוה kept for Himself to oversee. Genesis 15:18, *In the same day the Lord made a covenant with Abram, saying, Unto thy seed have I given this land, from the river of Egypt unto the great river, the river Euphrates*: (KJV) This land remains special to יהוה and He will make certain that the children of Abraham will dwell there.

Today, there are more than two hundred recognized nations in the world. This is a result of the division of the original seventy through war, land deals or various other reasons that people choose to separate themselves. recognizing the geographic areas of which a particular divine being rules can be difficult. There is an example of a divine being who rules over an area in the Bible. Daniel 10:12–13, *Then the man said to me, "Daniel, do not be afraid. Some time ago you decided to try to get understanding. You wanted to be humble before God. Since that time God has listened to you. And I came to you because you have been praying. But the prince of Persia has been fighting against me for 21 days. Then Michael, one of the most important angels, came to help me. He came because I had been left there with the king of Persia*. (ICB) Some things should be obvious but will be noted, The one who is speaking to Daniel is Gabriel. This is the same Gabriel who spoke to Zacharias in Luke 1:19, *And the angel answering said unto him, I am Gabriel, that stand in the presence of God; and am sent to speak unto thee, and to shew thee these glad tidings*. (KJV)

Also what needs to be understood is that the *prince of Persia,* is not a human prince. What human could withstand a messenger from the throne room of יהוה? Because the divine being was holding Gabriel back from Daniel, we know that this divine being had become disloyal to יהוה. That means the majority of the people living in that area had rejected יהוה. The evidence if that is throughout the book of Daniel whenever we read about how the people were so eagerly willing to bow to anything the king wanted.

The adversary doesn't need humans to be loyal to him, he doesn't even need humans to do what we may consider to be evil acts. The only thing the adversary needs to gain more authority over the geographic areas is for humans to be distracted, to look away from יהוה and believe the lies we have inherited. Conspiracy theorist keep pointing to the wealthiest elite and accusing them of domination through the One World Order when the elite are being used by the adversary as a scapegoat for his action.

Major world religions are not exempt from guilt in their role either. Much of Islam condones terror, Buddhists and other far East religions bow to idols and false [g]ods. Christianity may be the ultimate culprit. Catholic and Protestant doctrines convince Christians they can worship when they choose, how they choose and where they choose. Some Christian doctrines condone abortion, homosexuality and many pastors have been caught in adultery. Other doctrines allow Christians to work when they want, take their sabbath when they want, eat what they want while the entire time claiming to love אלהים. When we get to choose what is right or wrong, when we choose when we work or rest or what we eat we no longer are choosing to listen to יהוה and follow His instructions. When we choose to make ourself our אלהים we have replaced יהוה with self and that is when the divine being are unbound from their loyalty to יהוה and are free to stand in defiance against Him and against us.

The New World Order that so many around the world were afraid of is quickly approaching reality and sadly this was made possible by some of the very people who were trying to stand against it. In their defense, they thought they were doing the right thing but they had believed the lies. Much like the people living when the prophet Amos was alive, they thought they were serving יהוה until the warning we read in Amos 5:18, **Woe unto you that desire the day of the LORD! to what end is it for you? the day of the Lord is darkness, and not light.** (KJV) Many want the Messiah to come and rule with his rod of iron but they are calling down judgement on themselves. All the while the adversary is laughing at mankind, laughing because we have believed the lies we have inherited.

Thankfully the New World Order will be short lived, the adversary doesn't need it to last. The divine beings who betrayed their loyalty to יהוה will be dealt with severely, their death sentence is secure. This New World Order may be short but it will be destructive. Matthew 24:21–22, **For then shall be great tribulation, such as was not since the beginning of the world to this time, no, nor ever shall be. And except those days should be shortened, there should no flesh be saved: but for the elect's sake those days shall be shortened**. (KJV) While this speaks directly to the great tribulation, there is a great probability that the New World Order is part of this tribulation. Some Christian doctrines teach that Christians won't see the tribulation because they will be raptured away before it begins. For those, read the above passage again and again until you can answer who the elect are. The elect are the believers who are still alive, the ones who had properly prepared and survived as an example for the rest of the world. The pre-tribulation rapture is a lie that some have inherited and it can not be proven in scripture but there is plenty of evidence that believers will live through the tribulation.

Once the New World Order and the tribulation is finished, the rule of יהוה on earth will begin again. He will establish His instructions again to salvage as much of mankind as possible. Zechariah 14:16, ***And it shall come to pass, that every one that is left of all the nations which came against Jerusalem shall even go up from year to year to worship the King, the LORD of hosts, and to keep the feast of tabernacles.*** (KJV) This takes place after the fall of the New World Order and the tribulation during the reign of the Messiah on this earth. The feasts of יהוה will be reestablished as will all of the covenant from Mount Sinai.

What happens next is truly amazing, a new orderly world. This time, a new heaven and a new earth. Isaiah 65:17, ***For, behold, I create new heavens and a new earth: and the former shall not be remembered, nor come into mind.*** (KJV) After evil is finally defeated forever, יהוה will create the new heaven, exactly perfect and the new earth, complete with the new Jerusalem. Victory can be exciting to look forward to, but there is no way to claim victory without conflict. Before anyone can claim victory, victory must be accomplished. To defeat the adversary, we must be prepared. As with any team or military unit, you need to look like the other members. In the realm of believers that means living a Biblical lifestyle and that means following the instructions we have been given by יהוה. If you are not willing to do that, you are playing for the loosing team. There are no gray areas with this, either you're standing in the light or in the dark. How many analogies will be necessary for everyone to understand?

This new orderly world will be free of the curse that was placed on the original creation. Revelation 22:3, ***And*** *there shall be no more curse: but the throne of God and of the Lamb shall be in it; and his servants shall serve him* (KJV) There is a question that demands an answer in the preceding verses, Revelation 22:1–2, *And he shewed me a pure river of water of life, clear as crystal, proceeding out of the throne of God and of the Lamb. In the midst of the street of it, and on either side of the river, was there the tree of life, which bare twelve manner of fruits, and yielded her fruit every month: and the leaves of the tree were for the healing of the nations* (KJV) Why in a perfect place, where there are no more tears, death or sorrow (Revelation 21:4) would there be any need for healing?

The answer to this question requires extensive word study. The Greek word used in the Revelation 22:2 verse is θεραπεία, (ther-ap-i'-ah) Meaning care or attention. If this word sounds familiar it is where the English word therapy originates. Due to the evolution of the English language, our modern concept of therapy is not applicable to the definition we see in the Greek of the 1st century. The average modern person considers the word therapy mainly as a kind of counseling for a mental disorder of some type. However prior to modern medicine, therapy would have had a very broad spectrum of applications ranging from essential oils to chicken soup. Anything that wold have been considered nurturing and caring for another would have been described as therapy. To this end the *healing of the nations*, would be better translated as for the well-being or health of the people fortunate enough to find themselves living in the New Jerusalem.

Some who have written about this concentrate more on the word for the nations and attempt to separate the natural descendants of Abraham from the gentiles who have joined with them. Exodus 19:6, *And ye shall be unto me a kingdom of priests, and an holy nation. These are the words which thou shalt speak unto the children of Israel.* (KJV) The word nation in this verse is from the Hebrew גוי (goy) from which we have the more familiar word goy-eem (plural) or gentiles. In the new orderly world no separation of people would be necessary. There will be no different class of people, everyone will be recognized as necessary and beneficial for the skills they possess.

In the new orderly world, there will be no need to keep track of time as we do now. There will be no sun or moon to separate night from day, each period of time will be marked differently and we are not given any indication of what that will look like. One might speculate that you will know when you need to be somewhere because it will be written in your heart. Living in the New Jerusalem will not be sitting around playing a harp all day either. Revelation 22:12, *And, behold, I come quickly; and my reward is with me, to give every man according as his work shall be.* (KJV) In this future event is the promise that we will receive great things. Of course what could be greater than being a resident of the New Jerusalem? Yet above this is the promise of even more.

Preparing for any emergency that may happen is prudent, having built-in redundant contingency plans for what may go wrong can be wise as well. Many people have planned and prepared for the disasters that might have occurred but never manifested. Were these people foolish? The answer probably depends on perspective. During the cold war many people built bomb shelters and stocked them with the supplies necessary to survive a nuclear war. Thankfully that hasn't happened. Also during this time school children in the United States trained in air raid drills and other civil defense practices. Thankfully none of these things happened either. At the time these were wise practices, however looking back we can be glad the bomb shelters or the survival skills were never needed.

Looking forward, what should believers be preparing for? Ultimately believers should be preparing for life in the New Jerusalem! Many Christian doctrines promote faith alone is all that is needed to receive eternal life, but the Bible reads something different. James 2:19, ***Thou believest that there is one God; thou doest well: the devils also believe, and tremble***. (KJV) What do the devils know that causes them such fear, after all they believe don't they? Maybe they know what is written in Revelation 20:12, ***And I saw the dead, small and great, stand before God; and the books were opened: and another book was opened, which is the book of life: and the dead were judged out of those things which were written in the books, according to their works***. (KJV) Even the devils know were are not judged by what we say, we are judged according to what we do.

The caveat to being judged by what we do is that even if we simply do everything perfectly, but our heart is not loyal to יהוה, we risk blotting our name out of the book of life. 2 Chronicles 25:1–2, ***Amaziah was twenty and five years old when he began to reign, and he reigned twenty and nine years in Jerusalem. And his mother's name was Jehoaddan of Jerusalem. And he did that which was right in the sight of the Lord, but not with a perfect heart***. (KJV) Even though Amaziah did everything right, all of his actions were righteous, his heart was not loyal to יהוה. Just a short time later in verse 14, ***Now it came to pass, after that Amaziah was come from the slaughter of the Edomites, that he brought the gods of the children of Seir, and set them up to be his gods, and bowed down himself before*** *them, and burned incense unto them*. (KJV) Because his heart was not loyal, Amaziah bowed down to other אלהים blotting his name from the book of life and Judah had a difficult time during his reign. Finally Amaziah was killed and his body returned to Jerusalem.

What we learn form this is that we need to prepare our heart as well as our lifestyle. So important is having a heart loyal to יהוה that David writes in Psalm 44; 20–21, *If we have forgotten the name of our God, or stretched out our hands to a strange god; Shall not God search this out? for he knoweth the secrets of the heart*. (KJV) Even if our actions are not always right, when our heart is loyal to יהוה He will search out the secrets of our heart. One major Christian denomination teaches that if no one has ever been told about Jesus, they can not get into heaven. Hopefully these passages clarify that ridiculous notion. The אלהים who spoke and created this world is absolutely capable of knowing who is seeking to walk with Him. His mercy is so great that even when we get it wrong, we are still acceptable *IF* our heart is loyal to the one who created us, even though we may've never heard the name or forgotten the name יהוה.

SO WHERE DO WE GO FROM HERE?

Jacob was unsure about his relationship to יהוה. Jacob's ladder dream somewhere near Haran described in Genesis 28, is often portrayed as a wonderful heavenly vision but the reality is that Jacob woke up confused. He wondered what it had all meant and the only thing he knew for certain is that he was very close to יהוה and His house. Genesis 28:20–21, ***And Jacob vowed a vow, saying, If God will be with me, and will keep me in this way that I go, and will give me bread to eat, and raiment to put on, So that I come again to my father's house in peace; then shall the Lord be my God:*** (KJV) Jacob needed to know beyond any reasonable doubt that what he had seen in his dream had been from יהוה. Jacob wasn't testing יהוה, he was testing himself. Read the way this is written, if I'm going the way that אלהים wants me to go, He will feed me, clothe me and return me safely to my father's house. If any of those parameters are not met, Jacob would know he was not following the instructions from יהוה.

We do learn later that Jacob actually was going the right way and his relationship with יהוה was exactly as it should have been. Genesis 31:13, ***I am the God of Bethel, where you anointed the pillar and made a solemn vow to Me. Now get up and leave this land at once, and return to your native land.*** (BSB) Jacob returned to the land of his father with great anxiety. He even had another bad dream but when he met Esau his brother he realized he returned in safety. Yes, there was an issue with his daughter Dinah but bear in mind that was not right away.

What are we to learn from this? We learn that even when we are not certain if we are doing the right thing, if we are willing to test ourselves with reasonable parameters, יהוה will abide by those parameters. A short personal note, many years ago I did pray and say that יהוה created me with a hard head and a thick skin and that He had the permission to beat me over the head with a baseball bat if He needed to get my attention. A few days later I heard one of the most hard hitting messages I had ever heard. That message had been recorded many years before the day I heard it but I knew it was for me. The message revolved around Leviticus 23 and the appointed times we are to meet with יהוה and I can attest to this, that message got my attention.

Some people need to have that abrupt message, some only need a gentle nudge, some only need to hear a kind word from a friend. No matter what category you are in יהוה has a message for you and that message will seem like it is a personally engraved invitation to His throne room. For some, there will be the confusion and a need for a test, and that is OK. Many people in the Bible have tested themselves to be certain what they heard is the sacred word of יהוה not their own desire. Gideon threw out the fleece and

Ruth kept her mouth closed until she was spoken to. The question is what will you need?

What will you do with the information you have just received? Will you dismiss it? Will you argue with it using your traditions or doctrine? Or will you decide to dig into the sacred word of יהוה and discover what He wants you to find? What piece of the puzzle will you find?

When יהוה spoke and began to create, He developed a blueprint that was satisfactory for everything. The ground floor, to use that analogy, is the throne room in heaven, which may be the first thing He created, after all He would need a place to reign from. We could speculate that the next thing would have been the divine beings that would inhabit the heavenly realm. Of the divine beings two are described, the cherubim and the seraphim. The cherubs are not the cute little angelic creatures with small wings and a bow and arrow. These are the divine beings that have a more human type form. The description in Exodus 25:20, *And the cherubims shall stretch forth their wings on high, covering the mercy seat with their wings, and their faces shall look one to another; toward the mercy seat shall the faces of the cherubims be*. (KJV) describe a winged being with a face. Other places do not quite complete the description but give just enough information to consider a human form.

Ezekiel chapter 1 describes divine beings having four wings and cloven feet like a calf with the hands of a man also. The faces are described by the way they look. Most English translations describe each divine being having four faces, the face of a man, the face of a lion, the face of an ox and the face of an eagle. Maybe a more radical way to consider this is for Ezekiel to be explaining the appearance. When each looked in a direction or depending on the way their eyes and the facial features appeared they took on the appearance of these beings. Humans on earth today can take on the appearance of looking like these animals when they concentrate on something a certain way. Would considering that the eyes and the different facial muscles give the appearance of looking like a man or maybe like a lion when they are appearing majestic? Perhaps this concept isn't radical at all when we think of people having an appearance of strength like an ox or concentrating with fixed eyes on a target like an eagle.

Later in Ezekiel chapter ten he names the divine beings as cherubim, these are the same beings as chapter one. Yes, Ezekiel is describing the same thing and in fact in Ezekiel 10:22, ***Their faces looked like the faces I had seen by the River Kebar. Each creature went straight ahead***. (BSB) This is where Ezekiel is introduced in Ezekiel 1:1, ***In the thirtieth year, on the fifth day of the fourth month, while I was among the exiles by the River Kebar, the heavens opened and I saw visions of God***. (BSB) Ezekiel is not saying that he is remembering the vision, he is saying that it is the same vision that he is having again and describes it in more detail. The divine beings Ezekiel describes are not the engines that drive some unidentified spacecraft, these are cherubim that carry the throne of יהוה.

The blueprint that יהוה uses for the basic divine being is the same blueprint He uses for mankind. The exact fit and finish may appear different but the foundation is, for the most part, the same. After our last breath is exhaled on earth we do not magically wake up the next second in heaven as an *angel,* playing a harp on a cloud. That cartoon fantasy has propagated too long and too many actually believe that is what happens. Remember Paul's words in 1 Corinthians 15:22–23, ***For as in Adam all die, even so*** *in Christ shall all be made alive. But every man in his own order: Christ, the firstfruits; afterward they that are Christ's at his coming.* (KJV) The blueprint יהוה has established for mankind is to remain mankind. We will receive an incorruptible body upon resurrection but we do not turn into something other than what we are designed to be.

Maintaining Biblical Authority is the main focus of *God's Universe, God's Rules*[6]. Without Biblical Authority, mankind has no compass of conscience, there is nothing to indicate good or bad, right or wrong, righteous or evil. Only the code of conduct that יהוה embedded in His blueprint for His created beings determines what is acceptable behavior and what is not. When any created being begins to decide what is right or wrong for themselves, their lives and the lives of the beings around them begin the process of death. Without the compass of conduct that comes from יהוה there can be no integrity, honor or discipline to guide and direct our lives. We are then left to only self discipline self govern and self god. Left to our own devices, we will destroy ourselves.

The first to rebel was the Adversary, Satan, or whatever name you may want to use. His rebellion affected the divine beings around him. Eve's rebellion affected Adam and his rebellion affected all of mankind. After the death of Joshua and a great deal of idol worship, we read in Judges 17:6, *In those days there was no king in Israel, but every man did that which was right in his own eyes*. (KJV) יהוה Himself was to be Israel's king but the people rebelled, they lost their compass of conscience. The people had forgotten who יהוה is and what He had done for their fathers. The

---

[6]   God's Universe God's Rules, Jerry Mitchell, Christian Faith Publishing, Inc. 2017.

people were already beginning to inherit lies and pray to gods that can not answer.

Mankind's responsibility is to search out the truth, to find the answers that uncover the lies and to live the way we are designed to live as an example to the rest of the world. The most efficient means to accomplish that task is to reject manmade doctrine and tradition and embrace the instructions we received from יהוה. We were given the freedom of choice when יהוה breathed into Adam the breath of life. Genesis 2:7, ***And the Lord God formed man of the dust of the ground, and breathed into his nostrils the breath of life; and man became a living soul.*** (KJV) Without choice, we would not have the breath of life that gives us the ability to share ideas or enjoy the beauty of creation. Without the breath of life we would be no different than any of the created animals that react to stimuli rather than think through a problem. Because we are made in the image of יהוה and the other divine beings we are based on a blueprint that contains a code of conduct. When we reject that code we begin the process of death, but when we accept that code and adapt a lifestyle that exemplifies it, we have the opportunity for everlasting life.

The mixed multitude that made it to Mount Sinai was offered what could arguably be described as the greatest gift to any group of people. They were offered to opportunity to become a special treasure to יהוה Himself. A treasure He would consider so dear to Him that He would protect it as someone protects their own eye. That offer is extended to us today, if we are willing to hear His voce and obey His commands, we can be His people and He will be our אלהים.

WHO IS THE HIM IN JOHN 3:16?

T O   M A K E   T H E statement that John 3:16, ***For God so loved the world, that he gave his only begotten Son, that whosoever believeth in him should not perish, but have everlasting life*** (KJV) is probably the most quoted Bible verse by Christians, would most likely not be an exaggeration. When we remember that this verse is found while ישוע is chastising Nicodemus for not understanding the foundations of Genesis and put everything back into the context of transmitting important information, we need to ask ourselves who the *him* in this verse refers back to. Many would say the *him* is referring to ישוע however there are some basic rules of grammar that may or may not apply to that.

One needs to remember that the actual conversation between Nicodemus and ישוע would have been in Hebrew. There is nothing in the Bible to indicate that John was there to actually record the exact conversation, but there is sufficient detail to show if he was not there he has intimate knowledge of what was said. John's letter would not have been written to the gentiles, John uses the feast of Passover to show who ישוע is and what his purpose is to the Jewish community. Therefore we could successfully argue his letter was to the Jewish community and would have been first written in Hebrew and later translated into one of the Greek forms we have knowledge of today.

Because the Greek construct of the verse is all we have grammatically, we are able to use the other gospels as a guide for how ישוע refers to himself, we can conclude that the *him in John 3:16 refers to יהוה and not ישוע*. Reading the him now as יהוה maintains the monotheistic Hebraic mindset that is completely congruent with the Torah and the prophets. To replace יהוה with ישוע in this verse implies a polytheistic Greek mindset that is completely out of character for the way that ישוע speaks of himself or teaches others.

Remember Isaiah 12:2, ***Behold, God is my salvation; I will trust, and not be afraid: for the Lord Jehovah is my strength and my song; he also is become my salvation***. (KJV) יהוה offers the blood of ישוע, the only one of a kind hybrid between a divine being and a human as payment for the redemption of what was already His. Yet according to ישוע, the one who believes in יהוה will not perish but have everlasting life. ישוע reminded Nicodemus of this as he was speaking to him, we don't see it in the English but the way the Greek reads, the implication is there.

The very name ישוע, means יהוה is our salvation, Every day ישוע is reminded of who he needs to depend on because of his own name. The event we read about in Luke 2:46–47, ***Finally, after three days they found Him in the temple courts, sitting among the teachers, listening to them and asking them questions. And all who heard Him were astounded at His understanding and His answers***. (BSB) describes a young man who has a grasp of the Torah and prophets that would be unparalleled for that time. As alluded to earlier, *THE PROPHET* would have this capability however a ruling monarch would most likely not be so endowed.

John's abrupt end to the conversation does seem odd, one could consider that either ישוע was interrupted or that the actual ending to the conversation was not worthy of record. Either way, once again ישוע is pointing to יהוה as the authority, not to himself. In the next verse, John 3:17, **For God sent not his Son into the world to condemn the world; but that the world through him might be saved.** (KJV) the question should be what is the world and how is it to be saved? These of the Greek word κόσμος, (kosmos) cosmos in English here does not refer to the outer reaches of our universe. By definition the Greek word κόσμος means an ordered system, and used in this context mankind is that ordered system. יהוה sent ישוע among mankind so they should have the opportunity to escape the coming wrath of יהוה by following the example and teaching of ישוע who continually upheld the monotheistic oneness of יהוה.

A legitimate argument could be made that the use of the generic titles God and lord have added to the confusion and polytheism so rampant in Christian churches today. As stated earlier, this is one of the reasons for using the Hebrew names יהוה and ישוע, so they are more easily kept separate and independent of each other. The well overused English word lord has confused and conditioned Christians to accept lord as LORD in their English Bibles. When Christians read Romans 10:9, **that if you confess with your mouth, "Jesus is Lord," and believe in your heart that God raised Him from the dead, you will be saved.** (BSB) they have been trained to equate Jesus with יהוה. However when read in the proper context and with the correct understanding of the Hebrew word אדון (adōn) one would realize that the definition of אדון is not equivalent to יהוה but instead used as a title of respect and reverence much like addressing someone as master or sir. Not to reduce or remove the important position of ישוע, he is only the conductor and engineer, it is יהוה who actually owns the train.

There is a perfect example of this in Genesis 18, in verse 1, יהוה appears at the tent of Abraham. In verse 3 Abraham speaks and in some translations the word lord is capitalized indicating the use of the proper name יהוה. the problem is that is not what is found in the original Hebrew and Abraham would know better than to address יהוה so informally. Instead Abraham uses אדוני, (Adonē) literally my lord. This term of respect could today also be translated as sir, much like a soldier would address a senior officer. The term master typically indicate a slave or servant type of relationship in a negative way today, however in the past it was also used as a term of great respect. Abraham would never be so presumptuous as to say, *Hey* יהוה *come on in,* and neither should we.

Reading John 3:18 without the preconditioned, polytheistic traditions and doctrines becomes more evident that ישוע is again redirecting our focus onto יהוה. ***He that believeth on him is not condemned: but he that believeth not is condemned already, because he hath not believed in the name of the only begotten Son of God*** (KJV) The one who believes on יהוה is not condemned but the one who does not believe rejects the meaning of the name ישוע, which is, יהוה is our salvation. ישוע finishes his chastisement of Nicodemus when he began, in Genesis. John 3:19–21, ***And this is the verdict: The Light has come into the world, but men loved the darkness rather than the***

Light because their deeds were evil. Everyone who does evil hates the Light, and does not come into the Light for fear that his deeds will be exposed. But whoever practices the truth comes into the Light, so that it may be seen clearly that what he has done has been accomplished in God. (BSB) Reminding Nicodemus that יהוה spoke and created light, before the sun, to demonstrate that His glorious light will expose everything. Some people hat the fact that their evil will be found out and they hate יהוה for that but there are people in the world who do love and their love will be rewarded. The people who reject and hate יהוה will have no place in His kingdom, they will be left out and will be forgotten forever when the new heaven and new earth are established.

When Nicodemus came to visit ישוע, he had seen the things ישוע had been able to do. ישוע surprises Nicodemus with a statement that seems to catch him off guard. John 3:3, *Jesus replied, "Truly, truly, I tell you, no one can see the kingdom of God unless he is born again."* (BSB) The use of the English words born again are not consistent with the rest of the explanation. Conceived again would be a better and more accurate description of what ישוע is describing. Nicodemus questions how someone can be re-conceived because he knows a person can not return to the womb. There was at this time a growing Greek religious belief in rebirth, had ישוע used that description, Nicodemus would have questioned the intent ישוע had but the concept of re-conception was unheard of. This is what prompts Nicodemus to ask about re-entering the womb.

As ישוע continues, he tells Nicodemus that we must be conceived of water and spirit. These are the two parents we need in which to be conceived, if we desire to enter the kingdom of heaven. Many Christians today will use this as the basis for baptism, however in baptism we remain flesh and bone which can not inherit the kingdom. 1 Corinthians 15:50, ***Now this I say, brethren, that flesh and blood cannot inherit the kingdom of God; neither doth corruption inherit incorruption.*** (KJV) and 2 Samuel 12:23, ***But now he is dead, wherefore should I fast? can I bring him back again? I shall go to him, but he shall not return to me***. (KJV)

This foundational concept is found in Genesis, 1:6, ***And God said, Let there be a firmament in the midst of the waters, and let it divide the waters from the waters***. (KJV) This firmament is a part or portion of the spirit of יהוה that separates the waters between heaven and earth. This is the best physical description we are offered for a spiritual reality. ישוע describes our passing through this as a re-conception and like the wind that blows we don't know when or where anyone else is going. Some will eventually find themselves living eternally on the new earth while others will be in the lake of fire. When ישוע confronts Nicodemus with the reality that he doesn't understand genesis he begins to chastise him for his lack of knowledge in this fundamental impression but to give Nicodemus some credit, the shadow pictures for this had already been destroyed long before he was born.

Some may think it is unfair for ישוע to scold Nicodemus for teaching others to drive when he has never even seen a car but Nicodemus needed to hear in a way that was certain to make him understand. The interaction between the two makes them appear familiar with each other. One should consider the possibility of Nicodemus being present as a twelve year old ישוע was in the temple courtyard astounding the teachers of that day. Nicodemus is recorded by John as being one who brought herbs to anoint the body of ישוע, John 19:39, ***Nicodemus, who had previously come to Jesus at night, also brought a mixture of myrrh and aloes, about seventy-five pounds***. (BSB) The short interaction recorded offers insight into spiritual realities that most fail to contemplate. The reaction and response to the meeting in John 3 with Nicodemus should make one pay close attention to events as the writers of the gospels detail the acts and comments of the Pharisees. There may be hiding in plain sight glimpses of Nicodemus and others who were not as afraid fo ישוע as they were fearsome of יהוה.

What we learn from the encounter between ישוע and Nicodemus is that Nicodemus was familiar enough to feel comfortable visiting ישוע at night. This meeting held some extremely important details concerning creation and how we need to be prepared to leave this world. We also find that ישוע is consistently teaching others to focus on יהוה and not on other people. The most important lesson we learn is that when we reject the lies we have inherited and rely on sound Biblical authority and principle combined with etymology and forensic application of the clues found throughout scripture, יהוה becomes more glorious and more majestic.

EVOLUTION IS A HUMAN CONDITION

Perhaps the greatest lie we have inherited is the theory of evolution because it directly conflicts with the introduction to the sacred word of יהוה, **In the beginning אלהים.** Prior to beginning of the 18th century the majority of people including scientists believed the Biblical account of creation. Sir Isaac Newton (1642–1726) studied at Trinity College, Cambridge and was expected to become an ordained priest. Newton received special permission from Charles II to avoid that requirement in order to pursue his mathematical studies. This was also about the time the *Age Of Enlightenment* was beginning. The dangerous combination of science and philosophy allowed for the illusion that man had the ability to change the created laws of nature, the very blueprint יהוה used to design our physical universe.

About this time men such as James Hutton (1726–1797) known as the founder of modern geology were being influenced by this enlightened time. Hutton, first believed the earth was around six thousand years old as Archbishop James Ussher (1581–1656) of Ireland calculated using the genealogies found in the Bible. Hutton is also recorded as believing that fossils were the remains of animals that died during the flood of Noah. The philosophical influence at that time did not challenge us to seek the truth, instead philosophy during the *Age of Enlightenment* challenged us to question everything. Hutton, under this influence began to question what he believed to be geologic layers caused by the flood of Noah and began to introduce these as sedimentary layers that accumulated over time. Hutton developed a theory for the process he interpreted and writes, "The result, therefore, of this physical enquiry, is that we find no vestige of a beginning, no prospect of an end." This theory is quite contrary to what he had previously believed in that he completely removes any form of אלהים from the creation of the earth.

Hutton was not alone in this new way of thinking, Niels Steensen (1638–1686) and Comte de Buffon (1707–1788) had their own ideas of how the earth was *formed* instead of created. Most of the enlightened scientists had studied in theological institutions and yet they were influenced by the philosophy of their day and taught to question everything, including אלהים. Primarily these men worked in geology, attempting to attribute what they came to believe as millions of years of time to cause sedimentary layers to form into what they were observing on their explorations.

Alexander Von Humboldt (1769–1859) is another scientist influenced by his enlightened contemporaries. Humboldt's extensive exploration in the western hemisphere gave him access to view not only the geologic formations, he was amazed by the wide varieties of plants as well. He is noted for his book *Kosmos*[7] in which he attempts to bring the different sciences together. Humboldt was also among the first to suggest that man was able to influence or affect the earth in a negative way. He noted that changes in the climate may be caused by agricultural and industrial practices. One of Humboldt's experiments was with frogs. He would use various metals to see if there would be any reaction and apparently one day the moisture from his breath cause a frog to jump. Humboldt wrote, *it was like breathing life into a leg.* This event occurred in 1797 which makes one wonder if this was one of the inspirations for Mary Shelley's novel *Frankenstein* in 1818.

The enlightenment philosophy was not only influencing science and science fiction it has a profound affect on the church. With so many people beginning to question the age of the earth to be more than the six thousand years that is found in the Bible, they didn't realize what they were really asking is, *Did אלהים really say?* The same question the serpent asked eve, the same question that caused the fall of mankind. How could the church respond to the enlightened scientists of the day when the people could look at the earth and think—*IT LOOKS OLD.*

The foundation of the Bible had been questioned by the modern philosophy of the enlightened age. The response of the church was not to stand firm on the sacred word of יהוה, instead it attempted to insert millions of years into creation with what is known as the *gap theory.* Basically this theory states that between day 1 and day 2 of creation are millions of years of time or that each day is a thousand years based on Psalm 90:4, ***For a thousand years in thy sight are but as yesterday when it is past, and as a***

---

7 Kosmos, Alexander Von Humboldt, 1845.

watch in the night. (KJV) And 2 Peter 3:8, **But, beloved, be not ignorant of this one thing, that one day is with the Lord as a thousand years, and a thousand years as one day.** (KJV) Neither of these verses reveal that time is actually different in the heavenly realm but are figures of speech to indicate that time in the presence of יהוה should not be counted as we count time. Much like spending an enjoyable day with good friends that ends too soon, time with יהוה passes without notice. Nowhere in the Bible will it elude to time being calculated any differently than what we consider normal. Certainly Daniel didn't wait for twenty-one thousand years for Gabriel to deliver the message in Daniel 10:13, **But the prince of the kingdom of Persia withstood me one and twenty days: but, lo, Michael, one of the chief princes, came to help me; and I remained there with the kings of Persia.** (KJV) Only in Genesis chapter one is the argument for adding time to a day attempted and for the astute Bible student that attempt fails.

Never-the-less, the church allowed the influence of philosophy to creep in and then some actually began to teach the ridiculous *gap theory*. John Fleming (1785–1857) wrote that the flood of Noah was peaceful and left no lasting geographic evidence on the earth. Other pastors were preaching that we need to accept the millions of years of time. Even Charles Spurgeon (1834–1892) writes, *Can any man tell me when the beginning was? Years ago we thought the beginning of this world was when Adam came upon it; but we have discovered that thousands of years before that God was preparing chaotic matter to make it a fit abode for man, putting races of creatures upon it, who might die and leave behind the marks of his handiwork and marvelous skill, before he tried his hand on man.* Spurgeon, who has been considered the preacher's preacher allows for death before Adam on earth to conform to the *gap theory* in direct contradiction with the sacred word of יהוה.

With this new and enlightened philosophy replacing creation based theology, Charles Darwin (1809–1882) advanced mankind to the next level of thinking, not only is the earth millions of years old but mankind wasn't created but evolved over thousands of years into what we have become. Darwin who himself was raised as a Christian was heavily influenced by his peers in the Plinian Society while at the University of Edinburgh. Their discussions on the natural sciences obviously guided by the philosophy of the day led Darwin to abandon the religion he knew and the result is the religion of evolution we know today.

As Darwin traveled on the HMS Beagle, he was reading the books recently written by Humboldt and others concerning the geology of the earth. Darwin began to observe adaptations of animals and interpret those adaptations as slowly evolving changes. While he was quite astute at observing nature, his philosophic influence cause him to cross contaminate the geologic work of Humboldt with his biological observations and theorize that only the most fit and strong biological creatures survive. These survivors then evolve into the animals he was so carefully studying on his journey. Darwin semi-plagiarized the work of Humboldt's work in geology and adapted it to his own work with biology. Literally we have inherited lies within stolen lies.

Darwins book, *On the Origin of Species by Means of Natural Selection, or the Preservation of Favoured Races in the Struggle for Life,* Is a poorly interpreted observation of mankind's involvement with the world he lives in. Darwin sees no difference between animals and man, only that man has dominance over some animals through domestication. Darwin's implication that a species can be crossbred enough to produce a completely different outcome has failed miserably in real life. Of all of animals and plants that have ever been crossbred either domestically or organically a dog is still a dog, a cat is a cat and a rose is still a rose. Nothing mankind has ever done has resulted in a new species. No fossil ever found has indicated a transition of species. There is no possible way to crossbreed any selection of tomato plants and expect to grow anything other than a tomato.

The reproductive process of man and animals insists on maintaining the *kind*. Described in the Bible are animal kinds, while we may not have pictures of these first kinds of animals we can be sure that the dog kind had the genetic information that all dogs possess today. The cat kind had all of the genetic code for the cat breeds we see and so on. While crossbreeding within a kind is possible and adaptation to the environmental surroundings does occur, no new kind has ever been observed and no transition has ever been located. To consider a scaled reptile having the ability to reproduce and have a mutant bird with down hatch from an egg is simply science fiction. To pretend that could happen, to perpetuate the new species, that exact mutation would need to happen at least twice in the same geographic location with one being male and one female to have any hope at reproduction. Without reproduction the mutant species would die.

Secular scientists have been grasping at any hint of imaginary evidence to prove the theory of evolution. The sacred word of יהוה reveals that theory to be nothing more than the illegitimate imaginations of men rebelling against their Creator for their own personal profit. Real science must be observable and repeatable. Philosophic challenge is not science nor is it productive. The philosophy of the enlightened age has done nothing to advance the existence of mankind but it has interfered with mankind's relationship with יהוה. Because the church has allowed the philosophy of the enlightened age to pervert the sacred word of יהוה, it has failed in the very service it was designed to perform, to bring believers together for the benefit of all. The church by accepting millions of years of creation and death on earth before Adam has lost any credibility it may have had with the world. Today believers fight to recover the creation lesson we have in the Bible. Christian and Jewish scientists and archeologists are forced to add years to their findings to be considered credible. Adding time to the Bible destroys the timeline of earth's history causing confusion. All of this adding to the lies we have inherited from our fathers.

Believers must be willing to challenge the challengers, we can prove the history found in the Bible is real if you are willing to listen. Job is the most scientific book in the Bible. Job 12:7–9, ***But ask the animals, and they will instruct you; ask the birds of the air, and they will tell you. Or speak to the earth, and it will teach you; let the fish of the sea inform you. Which of all these does not know that the hand of the LORD has done this?*** (BSB) The problem with the enlightened scientists was they were challenging יהוה when they should have been smart enough to challenge themselves. They acted as אלהים insisting that they were smarter and better as the created than יהוה who created them. They held their ideas above the sacred word of יהוה and insisted that they were right and יהוה was wrong. They looked at the earth and claimed we know more than you do when Job said, *Speak to the earth and listen.* Like spoiled children the scientists of the enlightened age wanted to do things their way and today we are paying the price because the believers failed to resist.

The church took on a completely different persona as the philosophy of enlightenment dictated its' path. Instead of being set apart and Holy, the church began to look more like the secular social clubs of the day. Blending in with other worldly and cultural views the church began to be even more divided when unity would have been more productive. Most worship communities today resemble their secular surroundings. Instead of being an example to the world, they have become like the world. Their traditions and doctrines look eerily familiar to those of their secular counterparts. No one seems to be exempt from this odd form of inclusiveness. Atheists celebrate Christmas and Jewish homes are including a Hanukkah bush. (More on that later) יהוה instructs believers to be set apart for Him, not to look like or act like the rest of the world but to bring the world back into the family of יהוה.

Christian schools are mandated to teach evolution but public schools are practically forbidden to teach creation. Tax dollars in the United States are being used to promote the millions of years with paleontologists on some state payrolls driving to schools specifically to teach millions of years of evolution. These are nothing other than state sponsored preachers for their religion, converting more children into the philosophy of enlightenment through evolution. The very people paid to educate children have instead chosen to pervert their minds with the lies we have inherited. Education is about proper instruction, not promoting a false narrative to influence a way of life. Sadly most of the world has chosen to adopt this lie as truth and the price we are paying is evident, a society in need of יהוה who can not listen to the prayers delivered to the other אלהים that have replaced our Creator.

Much of mankind has completely adapted to the human conditioning of evolution that has been forced into the churches and synagogues around the world. Secular science has refused the reality of the sacred word of יהוה accusing it of being a fairytale to cover the lies of philosophical enlightenment. The entertainment industry has helped to promote the real fairytale of millions of years and evolution with books, movies and television shows depicting unrealistic dinosaurs and apelike cavemen afraid of fire. Secular scientist appear in front of lecture halls filled with people hoping to learn about the past but are filled with speculation and opinion. A fossil reveals how an animal died, not how the animal lived. When all we have are the bones, reconstructing the muscle and skin tissue for an animal no one has seen in almost a thousand years is mostly guesswork. No one really knows for sure what a T-Rex may have looked like. No one really knows what color the skin may have been and no one can say with any degree of certainty what they may have sounded like. All of that is artistic guesswork based on the similar reptiles alive today.

Evolution has evolved from theory to an elaborate hoax used in an attempt to discredit the Bible. Those who promote this religion may or may not realize they are acting exactly as the serpent in the garden. They are asking, *Did אלהים really say?* They are challenging יהוה and they are challenging each one who hears their message of philosophic enlightenment to choose between יהוה and some other אלהים. Remember the adversary doesn't care what אלהים you choose as long as you don't choose יהוה.

When the scribes asked which commandment was the first or greatest of all as detailed in Mark chapter 12:28–29, ישוע recites the Shema, Deuteronomy 6:4, ***Hear, O Israel: The LORD our God is one LORD*** (KJV) The scribes would most likely have been the Sadducees, the one who knew the legal aspects of the Torah the best, had ישוע changed any word of this they would have had ample ground to discredit him, here is this verse in a more appropriate format for this book;

Hear O Israel יהוה אלהים
יהוה is ONE

This should be sufficient evidence from the mouth of ישוע himself to prove the importance of who we are to worship.

Evolution may have caused more confusion among believers in the past two hundred years than any other single topic since the flood of Noah, including the tower of Babel. The number of people who have lived in the past two hundred years far exceeds the number of people who were present on the plains of Shinar to watch the tower fall. This massive attack against the very foundation of the Jewish and Christian faith has been overwhelmingly effective and the results are a continually decreasing number of people who believe the Bible is actually true.

While many people proclaim Christianity, many of those same people have also responded that they think the Bible is a book of good ideas but not everything in it should be taken as fact. They do not believe that אלהים really did say. They have fallen for the lies they have inherited. There is a concept being circulated among Christians that certain criteria may or may not be a *salvation issue*, evolution being among them. Because יהוה is our salvation (Isaiah 12:2) those who choose other אלהים or other religions such as the philosophy of enlightenment may have a very serious salvation issue.

Creation/evolutionists would have you believe that the earth was just formed and hanging around the solar system when יהוה came along and thought to Himself, *Here is a nice place to plop down some people.* Their gap theories or evolutionary nonsense can not stand the scrutiny of Biblical authority or real scientific experimentation. Everything from the geologic age of the earth to the ice age and the creation of man can be explained scientifically with observable and repeatable results. Archeology is producing amazing discoveries almost weekly that support the timeline we find in the Bible. Doctors are confirming that what we eat and how much exercise and work we do are directly connected to our health, confirming the dietary and work to rest instructions found in the the sacred word of יהוה, emphasizing that the one who designed us knows the best way for us to be healthy.

The philosophy of enlightenment is an extremely destructive force but it is not so destructive as to cause those who have a strong desire to walk with יהוה to waiver. Those who seek the face of יהוה as Moses did will be rewarded because He is יהוה he will not change so that those who choose Him are not destroyed. (Malachi 3:6) Hope is a strong emotion, it is equal to trust. When we trust יהוה and none other, we have nothing to fear. That lesson was lost to the church almost two hundred years ago. Perhaps, they will relearn what they have forgotten. Maybe they will understand they have inherited lies and attempt to find the truth.

REVISITING TRADITION

The Musical *Fiddler On The Roof*[8] gives us a glimpse into a culture filled with tradition. One of the most memorable scenes for many is when the character Tevye, Begins to sing the song, Tradition! As the traditions of his culture begin to melt away, Tevye, is faced with some difficult decisions, does he hold onto the traditions of the past that now seem to have no value or will he embrace the way his world is changing. Tevye puts up a good fight to maintain his traditions but in the end his world crumbles and he finally must face his reality and move on. So often we have our own fight to hold on to our traditions that we have embraced. Then when faced with the reality of the world we can try to hide from reality or ignore it but in the end we too, must move forward.

Some traditions can be fun, going on a vacation every year to the same place can be entertaining. Some traditions can be boring, visiting the same place year after year can get monotonous. Some traditions can be dangerous, running

---

8   Fiddler on the Roof: (from the Broadway Musical "Fiddler on the Roof"). [United States].

with the bulls is a tradition that has injured many over the years but it remains an annual event. Traditions depend on the individual to maintain them because traditions have no real value. Other traditions are dangerous because they become entwined with legends or myths and eventually are considered as truth. In the 21st century one can purchase a nativity scene with a drummer boy or a Santa Clause figure, neither were actually present when ישוע was born but it has apparently become tradition to include them.

Some traditions seem harmless until they become more important than the actual event they are meant to celebrate. Taking that annual vacation can be enjoyable until it becomes a burden. For believers accepting traditions or denominational doctrines as a replacement for the sacred word of יהוה is a very real and dangerous burden. ישוע warns of the dangers of maintaining tradition as scripture in Mark 7 and Matthew 15 records the same event. The tradition of washing ones hands before eating bread was considered more important than many of the instructions received through Moses. The response of ישוע in Mark 7:6–7, ***"Isaiah prophesied correctly about you hypocrites, as it is written: 'These people honor Me with their lips, but their hearts are far from Me. They worship Me in vain; they teach as doctrine the precepts of men."*** (BSB)

Of course ישוע is quoting from Isaiah 29:13, ***Therefore the Lord said: "These people draw near to Me with their mouths and honor Me with their lips, but their hearts are far from Me. Their worship of Me is but rules taught by men.*** (BSB) Isaiah's use of the word אדוני instead of יהוה in this verse has significant meaning. Isaiah chooses to speak for יהוה instead of quoting His words as Isaiah often does. Speculation is that יהוה was so furious that Isaiah wanted to tame this down. Others consider the use of אדוני to be a scribal error, which is plausible. Considering the surrounding text this verse begins the transition from wrath to reconciliation. The option for Isaiah to indicate how angry יהוה is at this point was to speak for Him because what יהוה really said was too harsh for us to hear.

Because ישוע chose to quote this from Isaiah with the possible understanding of how angry יהוה was, made the Pharisees and the disciples very nervous. So nervous that the Pharisees backed down and the disciples asked for clarification. This is lost to the Christians who don't actually study the language and culture of their Hebrew brothers and sisters and so the Christian attempts to make this about what food we are allowed to eat. The actual lesson in this passage is that mankind does not have the authority to replace the sacred word of יהוה with any added traditions. The word of יהוה is the word of יהוה and it will not change.

Tradition and legend are abundant concerning the death of Peter and Paul. Tradition is that Peter was crucified head down in Rome but there are no reliable writings in the Bible or extra Biblical material to confirm that theory. The *Acts Of Peter* is an extra Biblical writing that has not been verified as legitimate although many desire it to be. Supposed to have been written prior to the 3rd century AD and speculated that the early church father Origen was familiar with it. From this writing we are to believe that Peter was able to convince the Roman executioner to carry out his last wish to be crucified upside down while in Rome. All of this makes a very interesting tale, however there is nothing other than tradition and legend to justify this. Those who promote this theory rely on something ישוע told Peter in John 21:18–19, ***"Truly, truly, I tell you, when you were young, you dressed yourself and walked where*** *you wanted; but when you are old, you will stretch out your hands, and someone else will dress you and lead you where you do not want to go." Jesus said this to indicate the kind of death by which Peter would glorify God. And after He had said this, He told him, "Follow Me."* (BSB)

There is also the theory that Peter was executed in Jerusalem before he ever went to Rome. Acts 12:7, ***And, behold, the angel of the Lord came upon him, and a light shined in the prison: and he smote Peter on the side, and raised him up, saying, Arise up quickly. And his chains fell off from his hands.*** (KJV) As Peter is in prison bound in chains between two guards an angel strikes Peter in the side and he escapes. Later when Peter goes to the house of Mary, a young Rhoda sees him and is afraid. The story is white radical because the people in the house tell Rhoda she is seeing an angel. The main problem with Peter being killed while in a Jerusalem prison is that he appears at a meeting in Acts 15 and there seems to be no indication that meeting took place prior to acts 12.

Paul on the other hand could have been beheaded in Rome by Nero or he could have lived to a ripe old age in Spain. The legends and traditions of Paul's demise are equally absent of substantiated facts. Romans 15:24, ***I hope to see you on my way to Spain. And after I have enjoyed your company for a while, you can equip me for my journey.*** (BSB) This phrase in his letter hints that he fully expects to be released from his arrest in Rome and be on his way. Because the believed chronology of Paul's epistles places this about in the middle of his writing we can infer that Paul lived quite a while after writing it. Paul possibly did visit Spain and then Ephesus as some accounts indicate. Paul could have eventually gone back to Rome and would have been arrested again. This time Nero would not have been so forgiving as it was later enough when Nero was blaming the Christians and Jews for his trouble and Paul would have made a good scapegoat.

Widely overlooked is the probable reason for the uncertain resting place of Peter and Paul. Had the location of their tombs been known they very well could have become a pilgrimage destination. The polytheistic mindset of the Greco-Roman early gentile Christian would have attempted to turn Peter and Paul into more than they were. We see this in Christian denominations as people pray to Mary and we see the thousands of people each year at St. Peter's Basilica. So many people have kissed the toe of this statue it has worn down. Imagine how many more visitors would be making those pilgrimage treks if the actual tomb locations were known, not to mention how mush more divided believers would be as they argued over who was the better apostle. The current division creates an unhealthy spiritual conflict among believers with nothing more than a few written words. Having people fight over who's bones held the most healing spirit would be disastrous.

Some traditions have been a part of believers lives for so long they don't *feel* as if they are traditions. In the Jewish community the celebration of Hanukkah is surrounded by lights, latkes and dreidels. Ask most Jewish people why Hanukkah last for eight days and they will probably say because the miracle of the oil found in the Temple was only enough for one day but lasted for eight days. That's a great tradition with absolutely no historical record of substantiation. There are two places where the real reason for the eight day celebration can be read. 2 Maccabees 10:5–6, **It happened that on the same day on which the sanctuary had been profaned by the foreigners, the purification of the sanctuary took place, that is, on the twenty-fifth day** of the same month, which was Chislev. And they cele-brated it for eight days with rejoicing, in the manner of the feast of booths, remembering how not long before, during the feast of booths, they had been wandering in the mountains and caves like wild animals. Here we learn the eight day celebration was chosen because it would mirror the feast of Tabernacles or Sukkoth. There is no mention of any miracle of the oil, instead the entire lesson of deliverance is considered to be due to many miracles. A small nation such as Israel at the time defeating the mighty Greek army was unimaginable, but it happened.

Josephus writes much the same, *Antiquities Of The Jews* book 12, chapter 7; 323–325, **Now Judas celebrated the festival of the restoration of the sacrifices of the temple for eight days, and omitted no sort of pleasures thereon; but he feasted them upon very rich and splen-did sacrifices; and he honored God, and delighted them by hymns and psalms. Nay, they were so very glad at the revival of their customs, when, after a long time of inter-mission, they unexpectedly had regained the freedom of their worship, that they made it a law for their poster-ity, that they should keep a festival, on account of the restoration of their temple worship, for eight days. And from that time to this we celebrate this festival, and call it Lights**. Again no mention of any oil miracle. Had there actually have been an amount of oil that lasted, we should think it reasonable to be mentioned earlier in history than it is. While scholars don't agree completely, most admit the earliest mention of any oil associated with the rededication of the Temple is not written about until the 2nd century AD, approximately four hundred years after the event.

Today, Hanukkah is celebrated completely differently than it was in the past. Now because the Christian Christmas celebration is so near the same time as Hanukkah some Christmas traditions have found their way into Hanukkah. Exchanging gifts has become popular among the Jewish community as is the idea of erecting a small tree in the home often referred to as a Hanukkah bush. Candles and white lights have always been associated with Hanukkah but now the multicolored lights are used in some Jewish denominations as well. These traditions, as much fun and innocent as they may seem, have destroyed the memorial of the real miracles that happened which lead to the defeat of the Greek army. Hanukkah was a celebration of victory over evil, cleansing and rededication of corrupted vessels back into the service suitable for worshiping יהוה. Now it is reduced by many to be nothing more than a reason for another party.

For as much as Hanukkah has been influenced by Christmas, the Christians have created their own conundrums. Most Christians claim that Christmas is about celebrating the birth of *Jesus*, and yet they are the first ones to incorporate many of the pagan idols of Saturnalia or other pagan beliefs into their celebration. Some atheists today have also adopted the traditions of the pagans without even knowing it. The cultural cross influencing is an amazing phenomenon to observe with the trading of traditions and beliefs.

The practice of bringing a tree in to the home and decorating it was practiced as long ago as Abraham. One of the legends associated with Abraham is that he once asked someone why they would worship anything modern that glitters only temporarily. Some have used this legend to indicate the use of decorating a tree in the home which would die and need to be removed. Later Jeremiah would condemn the practice of cutting trees for the use of idols and while they were technically not Christmas trees, the custom of using a cut tree in the home was quite well known. In the 2nd and 3rd century Tertullian wrote against the use of cutting trees and bringing them into the home as a pagan practice. Some modern Christians use the excuse that they are not using the tree as the pagans did and they don't worship the tree. Others argue, *That's not what it means to me*, It really doesn't matter what it means to us, it matters what it means to יהוה. When He told Moses to write do not worship Me the way the pagans worship their אלהים in Deuteronomy 12, we should realize יהוה meant what He said.

Christians have chosen to celebrate the birth of ישוע at the same time the worshippers of Mithra were celebrating the rebirth of the sun. This did not happen by coincidence. The tradition that Constantine converted to Christianity is another lie we have inherited. What Constantine was able to do is create a hybrid religious system that he was able to control completely. Constantine was able to separate the Jewish followers of ישוע from the gentile followers by slowly removing any of the so called Jewish customs. The gentiles who were not familiar with why the Jews had an odd sabbath that lasted from sundown Friday until Sundown Saturday were content to follow Constantine's Sun-day sabbath. With each regulation further dividing the Jew from the gentile believer every appointed time or feast of יהוה was being erased from the mind of the gentile. Every shadow picture was being destroyed until the gentile believers themselves began to persecute the jews. Those fun traditions we use to celebrate loose their glitter and glamour when the twinkling lights are dimmed by the brightness that is the glory shining from the face of יהוה.

The birth of Christ was not an object of celebration until the fourth century. It was impossible to fix the date of the nativity, it was celebrated on the same day as the pagan Mithriac rights of the birth of the Sun and at the close of the Roman festival called the Saturnalia, held in mid December.[9]

When the Puritans settled in the United States, they forbid the celebration of Christmas as unChristian. Many northern colonies maintained this ordnance even after the American revolution. Christmas was not legally observed until 1836 and did not become a holiday until President Grant signed the bill into law on June 28, 1870 that made Christmas a legal holiday in the United States. This indicates that only a short amount of time is needed for a tradition or a legend to evolve from concept to an overwhelming explosive display of pageantry and decadency.

Not to be overshadowed the resurrection has also been corrupted by the lack of consideration for the appointed times of יהוה. The death, burial and resurrection follow precisely the events surrounding the Passover meal and the first fruits celebration. Due to Constantine's division of believers, the shadow picture of Passover was destroyed by the collusion of the resurrection with the orgasmic fertility celebrations of the Mithraic worshippers during the spring equinox.

Most holiday traditions the modern church celebrates can be traced to their pagan origins without a great deal of trouble if one is willing to sort through the layers of legend and lies we have inherited. Halloween and Valentines Day are not innocent of their influence either. Each and every one attempting to prevent the believer from discovering the truth that is to be found in the shadow pictures of the

---

[9]   From *The Layman's Bible Encyclopedia*, Southwestern Company, Nashville Tennessee, 1964 page 147.

Bible and experiencing the joy of having an intimate relationship with יהוה.

While not all traditions, doctrines or legends lead to the downfall of mankind, we must be constantly vigilant to maintain the lifestyle that יהוה designed us to live. Certainly celebrating a secular national holiday such as Independence Day, which is celebrated at various times of year in many nations can be enjoyed while glorifying יהוה who is responsible for allowing that to be a day of celebration. Remember that all of the leaders in the world are chosen by יהוה. Daniel 2:21, *He changes the times and seasons; He removes kings and establishes them. He gives wisdom to the wise and knowledge to the discerning.* (BSB) Even the leaders we may not enjoy are appointed by יהוה and He alone deserves our worship, as we celebrate the blessing He has poured out on us.

Extreme caution should be exercised while peeling back the layers of lies. Prayer and discernment are needed to recognize the difference between a blessing from יהוה and what may be something we desire from another source, especially if that other source is an unholy spirit. Reviewing our traditions to eradicate the empty, useless and meaningless distractions in our lives is no easy task. There are things we have a strong desire to hold onto because of special memories associated with them or perhaps they meant something special to someone close to us. When the traditions of our fathers cause us to sin, those traditions must be named for what they are and never allowed to influence us again. More importantly, teach your children that those traditions are sin and not to be repeated. Just as a bad tradition can become embedded in your life very quickly, living the way we are designed to live can quickly become your lifestyle as well. The choice is yours to make.

The complex composition of most traditions would make a blanket statement such as, *they're all bad*, incorrect. Each tradition needs to be evaluated on its' own merits according to Biblical authority, not our own individual desire. Someone being unfamiliar with the Bible may want to begin with the lesser traditions to examine before attempting to combat the more socially entrenched traditions such as those surrounding Christmas. Rome may not have been built in a day but it burned very quickly. The process should be to build up the kingdom of heaven, not to tear apart the family if you choose to live a more Biblical lifestyle.

Giving up long held traditions can be more difficult than an addict giving up their addiction. Challenging the doctrines you have trusted and finding they are inconsistent with the Bible is equally disturbing. Many people go through denial, anxiety and anger and that is normal. Learning the people you trusted had inherited the lies they passed on to you may feel devastating, but there is freedom in truth and the Biblical definition of truth is found in Psalm 119:142, ***Your righteousness is charitable and your instructions are <u>truth</u>***. (Jerry Mitchell translation) The same אלהים who at the completion of creation said it was very good, is the same יהוה who tells us through David that His sacred word is our standard for what is to be considered true and factual. That is not tradition, not doctrine and not legend, it simply is.

Those who reject the sacred word of יהוה saying it was for a different generation or that it has been done away or that does not bring life have little concept of how dangerous their reasoning is. For too many Christians their polytheistic traditions and doctrines have become their ultimate replacement theology, replacing יהוה with ישוע. With all of the Biblical forensic evidence to disprove any attempt of ישוע to replace יהוה but instead to uphold the majesty and glory of יהוה, there should be no doubt in anyone's mind that one of the greatest lies ever perpetrated on mankind is to question the sacred word of יהוה. Yes, יהוה really did say, and what He said is true.

WILLFUL IGNORANCE IS NOT BLISS

2 PETER 3:3–5, ***Knowing this first, that there shall come in the last days scoffers, walking after their own lusts, And saying, Where is the promise of his coming? for since the fathers fell asleep, all things continue as they were from the beginning of the creation. For this they willingly are ignorant of, that by the word of God the heavens were of old, and the earth standing out of the water and in the water:*** (KJV) We are no different today, we willingly forget the foundation of our faith, that is to trust only יהוה. When we attempt to replace His sacred word with our own desire we must pervert His word in order to make it fit our lusts. That is when the people in the Bible who lived real lives become only characters on a page. We read about the people in the Bible and fail to learn from their examples. Instead we burden the figures we read about in the bible with being great and larger than life. When we reduce the experiences of the people in the Bible who are our examples to nothing more than fictional

characters, we become willingly ignorant of the lessons in their examples. So when Hosea informs us that the people of his time were being destroyed because they had lost the truth and the love that comes with the truth, they were subject to loose the knowledge of יהוה as well.

Hosea 4:6, ***My people are destroyed for lack of knowledge. Because you have rejected knowledge, I will also reject you as My priests. Since you have forgotten the law of your God, I will also forget your children***. (BSB) Because there was not truth (the sacred word of יהוה) or mercy nor knowledge in the land the people were accused of wrongdoing by יהוה Himself. Those who reject His instruction can not serve as His priests, His representatives on earth. This is a harsh reality for many who have inherited the lies that teach any type of a prosperity gospel that can never be revoked.

Hosea 4:1, ***Hear the word of the LORD, people of Israel, for the LORD has a case against the inhabitants of the land: There is no truth, no faithful love, and no knowledge of God in the land***! (HCSB) The people had rejected the sacred word of יהוה and the result was there was no love or real knowledge of Him either. Their ignorance did not protect them from the anger of יהוה who watched as they prostituted themselves to the lesser אלהים. When all seems lost and the only solution to the problem is יהוה He is willing to receive the repentant. Hosea 6:1, ***Come, let us return to the LORD. For He has torn us to pieces, but He will heal us; He has wounded us, but He will bind up our wounds***. (BSB) Without any knowledge or love the people return and realize what has happened, יהוה allowed the people to reject Him if they wanted. The result of a life void of יהוה is meaningless and empty, Hosea describes it as being torn to pieces.

In the letter that John is told to write to the church in Ephesus ישוע accuses the church; Revelation 2:4, ***But I have this against you: You have abandoned your first love***. (BSB) Is he referring to Hosea's words and implying that because they have abandoned their first love they have also abandoned the truth? This warning comes with a solution; Revelation 2:5, ***Therefore, keep in mind how far you have fallen. Repent and perform the deeds you did at first. But if you do not repent, I will come to you and remove your lampstand from its place***. (BSB) Obviously there are some very strong similarities between the Hosea 4 passage and the letter to the church in Ephesus. Had they also become willingly ignorant of the foundation of their faith and replaced it with something else?

Paul's epistle to the Ephesians is filled with constant reminders of who they were and who they are. Ephesians 2:2, ***you used to walk when you conformed to the ways of this world and of the ruler of the power of the air, the spirit who is now at work in the sons of disobedience***. (BSB) Ephesians 2:19, ***Therefore you are no longer strangers and foreigners, but fellow citizens with the saints and members of God's household***, (BSB) Then in Ephesians 3:6, ***That the Gentiles should be fellowheirs, and of the same body, and partakers of his promise in Christ by the gospel***: (KJV) Now that you have been redeemed you are just like the mixed multitude that came out of Egypt, you have the chance to live the way that יהוה designed you to live.

The people were surrounded by polytheistic pagans who were constantly bombarding the new believers with insults for their conversion. the Jewish believers were of little help because they were fighting to maintain the rules of the pharisees and the Sadducees were attempting to discredit the possibility of the resurrection. What were the people in the fellowship of believers to do? Ephesians 4:1–3, ***As a prisoner in the LORD, then, I urge you to walk in a manner worthy of the calling you have received: with all humility and gentleness, with patience, bearing with one another in love, and with diligence to preserve the unity of the Spirit through the bond of peace***. (BSB) To put it another way, repent and help each other maintain a right relationship with יהוה and hold each other accountable for their actions.

Unfortunately too many of the the modern Christian churches today have fallen into the same trap the Ephesians did, they have allowed the influence of the world to guide their faith. The first love is abandoned and the truth, can not be found in them. They are being destroyed for lack of knowledge. They are willingly ignorant concerning the foundation of their faith. That is a harsh accusation but there is a more harsh accusation waiting for the other believers who failed to warn them that the enemy was inside the wall.

Ezekiel 3:18–19, ***If I say to the wicked man, 'You will surely die,' but you do not warn him or speak out to warn him from his wicked way to save his life, that wicked man will die in his iniquity, and I will hold you responsible for his blood. But if you warn a wicked man and he does not turn from his wickedness and his wicked way, he will die in his iniquity, but you will have saved yourself***. (BSB) Have the wicked been warned? Are the modern churches and synagogues who allow and encourage sin ignorant and lacking knowledge or are they ignoring the warnings and willing to destroy themselves? Have they accepted the lies they have inherited without testing them against the Bible? Maybe the question is, Who's responsibility is it to hold the church accountable?

Paul writes in 1 Corinthians 5 that we are to hold each other accountable. He writes that *it is reported* there is something going on and he then continues that just because he isn't there doesn't mean these things are to be allowed. Sin must be removed from the fellowship of believers, Genesis 17:14, ***And the uncircumcised man child whose flesh of his foreskin is not circumcised, that soul shall be cut off from his people; he hath broken my covenant***. (KJV) The one who violates the covenant must be exiled until repentance takes place and the evidence or repentance is observed. Does that seem drastic? Look around at the worship communities you may be familiar with. Has sin been allowed to permeate the body of believers?

1 John 3:4, ***Whosoever committeth sin transgresseth also the law: for <u>sin is the transgression of the law</u>***. (KJV)

Psalm 119:142, ***Your righteousness is charitable and your instructions (laws/ Torah) are truth***. (Jerry Mitchell translation)

To violate the sacred word of יהוה is to sin. Sin is not violating some man made rule or ordnance. If a Man makes a rule that no chocolate is allowed in his home and someone brings a gift of chocolate to him, that is not a sin. The normally appreciated gesture may be met with aggravation or even contempt but it is not a sin. This Biblical definition must be kept when addressing accountability among believers. When a particular denomination chose to adopt non-Biblical rules, those rules only apply to the members who agree to those rules. Some Christian denominations do not allow dancing or attending a movie or concert, violations of these doctrines can not automatically become a sin simply because they are incorporated into a religious organization.

A pastor for a conservative denomination was playing a lively rendition of a familiar hymn on the piano when he noticed someone in the front was tapping their foot to the beat of the music. The pastor immediately stopped playing and announced that he would not continue if it would cause someone to sin. In the pastor's mind tapping the foot constituted dancing, which was not allowed by that denominations doctrine. Apparently that denomination had not read how David danced with joy as the Ark Of The Covenant was brought into the City of David. 2 Samuel 6:16, ***As the ark of the LORD was entering the City of David, Saul's daughter Michal looked down from a window and saw King David leaping and dancing before the LORD, and she despised him in her heart.*** (BSB) But this is not the end of the story, because Michal, despised David for his display of joy for יהוה she suffered greatly. 2 Samuel 6:23, ***And Michal the daughter of Saul had no children to the day of her death.*** (BSB)

We are never given the authority to change the sacred word of יהוה, Deuteronomy 4:1–2, ***Hear now, O Israel, the statutes and ordinances I am teaching you to follow, so that you may live and may enter and take possession of the land that the LORD, the God of your fathers, is giving you. You must not add to or subtract from what I command you, so that you may keep the commandments of the LORD your God that I am giving you.*** (BSB) No matter how well intentioned, when we inject our own interpretations into the sacred word of יהוה, we corrupt His instructions.

The unintentional or even the uninformed sin is easily forgiven but the arrogant rejection of יהוה and being willfully ignorant are not. Leviticus 4:27–28, *"If anyone of the common people sins unintentionally in doing any one of the things that by the LORD's commandments ought not to be done, and realizes his guilt, or the sin which he has committed is made known to him, he shall bring for his offering a goat, a female without blemish, for his sin which he has committed.* (ESV) Unintentional sin does have a price, but that price is very minimal compared to the price of arrogance. Hebrews 10:26–27, *If we deliberately go on sinning after we have received the knowledge of the truth, no further sacrifice for sins remains, but only a fearful expectation of judgment and of raging fire that will consume all adversaries.* (BSB) Those who choose the God of Abraham will not accept the polytheistic view of the trinity—no one who claims to follow יהוה is able to also claim that ישוע is יהוה This is nothing more than polytheism that is allowed to infiltrate the society of believers in order to divide believers and create the replacement worship of יהוה for the worship of a different god.

Earlier scripture was used to provide prophetic evidence that ישוע will act as יהוה on the new earth. The prophetic and gospel writers never considered a polytheistic אלהים and the only testimony of such a belief is found in the writings of the polytheistic gentile early church fathers who attempted to throw away the foundation of their faith so they could have a religious system that suited their world view. The lies that we have inherited from them have allowed many to be willingly ignorant of the sacred word of יהוה. Some have become quite complacent in their faith and others have developed a crass attitude for יהוה, keeping Him in a holding pattern and considering Him their personal emergency responder and then wondering why He doesn't answer their plea for help.

Those early church writers are valuable for reference, however we must not allow ourselves to blindly stumble into the trap of becoming willingly ignorant of the foundation of our faith, found in the first five books of the Bible as some of those early church fathers did. In their eagerness to follow ישוע, they offered him more devotion than they offered to יהוה. While worshipping someone who was resurrected from the dead may be tempting, the resurrection did not make ישוע any more divine than it made Lazarus and no one worshipped him. The resurrection of ישוע holds more than we may ever realize, yes the person named ישוע was raised by the wonderful, awe filled and amazing power of יהוה and along with that, the meaning of the name is also resurrected: יהוה is our salvation.

Those early church fathers suffered from the same malady many believers suffer from today, the *Torah Syndrome* mentioned earlier. Jumping from one belief to the next trying to find where they fit into the equation. Exchanging one practice for another until exhaustion finally compels a pause for a breath. The early church fathers had no concept of what a messiah was or should look like, they didn't understand what the job a prophet was and certainly didn't know how to recognize *THE PROPHET.* Those who were truly searching to walk with יהוה will find their path but those who were not will continue their quest. Forcing an alternative concept into the Bible is exactly what the adversary desires. Remember the enemy doesn't need us to worship him or to do evil, he simply has a desire for us to live differently than יהוה designed us to live. Ignorance of the name, appointed times and commands of יהוה accomplishes the desire of the adversary.

Biblically speaking, the opposite of ignorance is knowledge. According to Hosea, the lack of knowledge or being willingly ignorant leads to destruction. The good news is that acquiring knowledge has the potential to build, more specifically the correct knowledge of יהוה allowed us to build a relationship with Him! A relationship built from desire is much stronger than a relationship based on need. We all need to eat healthy but for many, our desire is for dessert. יהוה has the ability to offer us a healthy dessert, not the kind of healthy dessert that causes a gag response when you taste it either. What יהוה has to offer us truly is sweet to the taste, light on the stomach and even narrow on the waist. Knowing and understanding יהוה is not complicated, learning to walk with Him is not strenuous and maintaining a relationship with Him is far more rewarding than imaginable.

For the ancient Hebrew culture, a curse meant to be weakened. the word ארר, (arar) reminds us the strength comes only from יהוה and we are nothing compared to Him. Shakespeare is credited with the words, "*Ignorance is the curse of God; knowledge is the wing wherewith we fly to heaven.*" This is closely associated with Proverbs 8:10, **Receive my instruction, and not silver; and knowledge rather than choice gold**. (KJV) The choice is clear from this ancient viewpoint, do we remain weak in our ignorance or do we enjoy the strength we receive through the knowledge of יהוה and His sacred word? All of the forensic clues we find in the Bible lead to the same conclusion, we can believe the sacred word of יהוה and trust Him and only Him.

the phrase *a little knowledge is a dangerous thing* may be familiar. If someone has limited knowledge of flight, should they be trusted to fly an airplane filled with people? Of course not. Yet there are theologians in the world who hold multiple degrees who are practically ignorant of what is really contained in the Bible. John 3:10, ***Jesus said, "You are an important teacher in Israel. But you still don't understand these things?*** (ICB) Even Nicodemus was ignorant about many things, the traditions and pharisaical doctrines had corrupted his understanding and his relationship with יהוה. Are the professors today any less susceptible to the lies they have also inherited? A better question would be to ask if they are teaching others to accept the lies rather than relying on the sacred word of יהוה? The only course is to navigate through the traditions, doctrines and lies that have been laid like landmines waiting to step on their trigger. Not to worry, there is a map for the minefield and it is knowledge that comes from the sacred word of יהוה. When Nicodemus came to ישוע, he didn't know he would be given a map to detect the traps of his day. A map that began in genesis and ends in the New Jerusalem.

Today we have access to that same map that ישוע gave to Nicodemus. We can choose to study and learn to understand through the eyes of the writers and see the traps and other bad choices we should avoid or we can choose to be blinded by the lies and wander aimlessly through our field tripping on traditions and being destroyed by our own doctrines. When we are searching for the chance to walk with יהוה, and trust Him, He will not be trapped by our traditions nor will He be deceived by our doctrine. We can be assured that our future, our everlasting life is secure when we choose to trust יהוה.

קצה

END/COMPLETE

WE ARE NOT designed us to sail through life without a compass, יהוה gives each of us certain skills and if we choose to use them our lives will be, productive, successful and joyous. His instructions are for our guidance and our well-being. Ignoring those instructions either through rejection or ignorance will result in a shortened, miserable life. Mentioned earlier is a compass of conscience, left to our own devices, mankind would self destruct. Thankfully there is a compass we are given, contained in the breath of life is a compass that points to יהוה as our Creator. Even the most remote villages ever discovered understood the most fundamental act for a society to exist; treat the ones around you the way you would want to be treated.

Evidence of this can be found in the relationships between the cannibalistic tribes around the world. Most, if not all are reported to have only eaten members of opposing tribes (or the occasional stranger who stumbled into their territory) but they rarely of ever killed one of their own members for consumption. Some of the South

American cannibal tribes would eat their relatives after death to absorb their spirits but that is different in that they were eaten after a natural death.

An inborn compass of conscience would prevent us from being capable of murder, theft, adultery or other offenses that would cause unrest between people. On our own we are self serving, typically looking out for only ourselves. The compass of conscience is the instructions we have been given by יהוה for how we are to live but He also gives us something that draws us to Him, In English we describe it as spirit although there is more involved than a single word can explain.

When יהוה said in Genesis 1:26, ***"Let Us make man in Our image, after Our likeness, to rule over the fish of the sea and the birds of the air, over the livestock, and over all the earth itself and every creature that crawls upon it."*** (BSB) We often get caught in the trap of who else was there, to this end there are two good explanations. 1, because the Hebrew word for the title of God is אלהים and it is plural, then for Moses to write I will create man in my image would be grammatically incorrect. for the second explanation I would suggest reading *A Commentary ON THE BOOK OF GENESIS PART ONE*[10] as Cassuto has a very good argument for this including the following verse. genesis 1:27, ***So God created man in His own image; in the image of God He created him; male and female He created them*** (BSB) This verse is completely singular, together we have the perfect image of an all encompassing Creator who is altogether one אלהים, plural and His name יהוה, singular.

---

[10]   A Commentary On The Book Of Genesis part one by Umberto Cassuto ©2005 Varda Books.

Our spirit has a desire to connect with the Spirit of יהוה and that is the compass, always pointing to יהוה, trying to guide our lives to Him. alone we will destroy ourselves but when our spirit has the opportunity to connect with the Spirit of יהוה, something supernatural happens. We learn the difference between right and wrong, we learn how to treat others the way we want to be treated and we learn what love really is and what it means to hold the needs of others above the wants of ourself. Simply put, when our spirit connects with the Spirit of יהוה we learn how to love and how to live. Placing the needs of others above our own desire does not usually happen naturally, that spiritual connection needs to occur for us to find the ability to love our neighbor as ourself. A compass only gives direction, a map is needed to show us where we are compared to where we want to be. The sacred word of יהוה is our map, His instructions are the course we should choose if we want a long, happy, healthy, productive and successful life.

יהוה never leaves anyone in the same or worse condition than when He first engages with them. Noah, settled a whole new world and his offspring are the people who are alive today. Abram was called across a river, Moses, rescued a nation. Even ישוע healed the blind, the sick and the crippled. We are responsible for the well-being of our fellow man… when our fellow man is willing to accept our help. We may wonder if Noah, Abram or Moses were the first choice for the jobs they were offered or if they were the first ones to say *Yes,* the reality is they accepted the responsibility and we will be forever grateful. Every day יהוה is asking the people who have accepted Him to reach out and be the example that someone needs to see. Not everyone can be an Abraham or a Moses but almost everyone can be a Ruth or Boaz. Some of us identify as Peter and others try to be like John. We should be encouraged to be the best person we can be.

The people we read about in the Bible have lived their lives in their time, now is our turn to live, learn, love and be the example for the next generation. Now it is our turn to dig through the language, the culture and the history to find the truth that is revealed to us in the sacred words of יהוה. To uncover the layers of lies we have inherited and to expose the אלהים of wood and stone that can not hear and will not answer and to teach those who accept יהוה as the Creator אלהים of Abraham, Isaac and Jacob as their אלהים. Then learn how to live the way יהוה designed us to live. Some may refer to this as a Torah driven life but it really doesn't matter what name you give it. When you choose to live the way that יהוה created you to live, your life will improve. When you understand that you need to invest in the kingdom of heaven and that investment does not include tangible worldly goods but a lifestyle that reflects who and what you place your trust in.

The parable of the talents in Matthew 25, describes 3 people who were given what their master thought they could be responsible for. The first two acted responsibly but the third hid what was given to him and earned nothing with it. The master considered him evil, useless and lazy and ordered him to be removed from his presence. The question is: what is your witness, what is your example and how are you investing in the kingdom?

Are you leading by example? Are others able to know you are a believer by watching you? Or do you resemble the rest of the secular world? Think before you answer these questions, look at your life, examine every aspect. When others look at you do they see someone who lives a life-style that reflects what they claim or do they see a hypocrite? If you claim to represent the Bible are you living that way or are you representing your traditions and doctrines? Someone once said, *Well, it really doesn't say in the bible but we believe…* that is the epitome of hypocrisy! Claiming to represent one thing and doing something different.

Luke 19:13. ***And he called his ten servants, and delivered them ten pounds, and said unto them, Occupy till I come***. (KJV) when this was translated into English the word *occupy* meant to take possession. When one possesses something they have responsibility for what they possess. Because you possess the knowledge of יהוה, you are responsible for more than taking up space! You have a responsibility to lead by example and to demonstrate to others that יהוה can be trusted to do everything He has said He would do. Are you living that way or are you living in fear? Is your spirit the compass that guides you too יהוה, connecting His Spirit to your spirit? Are you following the instructions that יהוה gave to us or do you try to justify and twist His words to suit your own pleasure? These are tough questions, and even more difficult when we realize we are probably guilty of sin more often than we want to be.

When we are willing to examine ourselves honestly, we will find that our actions do not always reflect the example we want to be. We all have shortcomings and we all have things in which we will excel. Peter is a good example of someone who had a difficult time overcoming his traditions. His love for יהוה and for his teacher ישוע, was great but the traditions and doctrines he grew up with kept him from being completely committed to either. Even after the crucifixion, Peter went back to what was familiar, he went fishing. John 21:3, ***Simon Peter saith unto them, I go a fishing. They say unto him, We also go with thee. They went forth, and entered into a ship immedi-***

ately; and that night they caught nothing. (KJV) *I'm going fishing*, one can almost feel the depression in Peter's voice when that verse is read. A conversation the next morning changed everything for Peter.

Do you love me? Three times Peter was asked this question. While many theologians have discussed the conversation in great detail. most have overlooked that this was the turning point for Peter. This conversation is where Peter finally gave up his traditions and chose to live the way he was designed to live. The result of this conversation was for Peter to give up the Pharisaical rules and follow the Torah, the sacred word of יהוה. Once Peter chose to use the map, his life changed dramatically. He was no longer stumbling around as a fisherman who happened to follow a certain teacher, now Peter had a destination and a map of how to reach where he needed to be. The same question asked three times, it could have been, *Are you certain you want this?* Peter never needed to return to fishing, this was his job interview. Much like Moses had the ultimate job interview with the voice in the burning bush to lead the people out of Egypt, the real question ישוע is asking Peter is, *Will you lead people to יהוה?*

Peter needed to abandon his traditions and the doctrines of the Pharisees in order to follow the map and reach his destination. The traditions and denominational doctrines we have today are really no different, they only look different, they are the same lies have been inherited and passed to the next generation. Believers today, both Christians and those practicing Judaism, must make the same choice Peter did. The question doesn't change, *Are you willing to live a lifestyle that leads people to יהוה?* Each of us may have a slightly different path we follow to reach our destination. Some may travel over land and others by sea but those last few steps lead through a very narrow gate and few are willing to find it.

Rejecting the centuries of lies that are so embedded in our legends, traditions and doctrines will offend some of the people you care about. While some Christians would consider this a form of persecution and embrace that as their cause, the over popularization of persecution has become an unhealthy trend in the Christian world. When ישוע was speaking in Matthew 16:24–25, ***"If anyone wants to come after Me, he must deny himself and take up his cross and follow Me. For whoever wants to save his life will lose it, but whoever loses his life for My sake will find it***. (BSB) Being persecuted was not a popular concept. The people living under Roman rule knew what real persecution is, they watched as the people around them were beaten and killed for violating the Roman civil laws. Would ישוע, who understood the sacred word of יהוה meant to preserve life have given such advice to his followers? Not the way think of that statement today if ישוע did speak these exact words. There are other references that allude to this concept being used. Earlier in Mathew 10:38, ***and anyone who does not take up his cross and follow Me is not worthy of Me***. (BSB) Interestingly not all of the manuscripts contain this verse and of the other verses that are similar, variations appear, however we can be confident that ישוע was telling his disciples there would be trouble should they choose to forgo their traditions and the rules of the Pharisees to follow the sacred word of יהוה.

This short forensic comparison reveals that there was at the very least a conversation about being pursued for walking with יהוה. When the disciples listened to ישוע early in his ministry he said in Matthew 5:10, ***Blessed are they which are persecuted for righteousness' sake: for theirs is*** *the kingdom of heaven*. (KJV) The word persecuted used here in Greek is διώκω (dee-o'-ko) and can mean persecuted or pursued. In the Hebrew gospel of Matthew we read exactly the same thing you will be pursued for seeking righteousness.

Matthew 10:34–36, ***Think not that I am come to send peace on earth: I came not to send peace, but a sword. For I am come to set a man at variance against his father, and the daughter against her mother, and the daughter in law against her mother in law. And a man's foes shall be they of his own household.*** (KJV) Here is where we **can compare ישוע to Mattathias Maccabee.** ***Drawing a line in the sand ישוע is repeating the famous words from 1 Maccabees 2:27, Then Mattathias cried out in the city, "Let everyone who is zealous for the law and who stands by the covenant follow me!" The difference is that the Maccabee's fought a war against the Greek army for their abomination of the Temple, ישוע was challenging the Jewish community to uncover the lies, abandon the traditions and the rules of the Pharisees that destroyed the shadow pictures established by יהוה at creation. Those same lies are still being inherited today, tradition and doctrine that conflict with the Bible are held more closely than the sacred word of יהוה.***

Christians will read this passage without realizing what ישוע is really saying—Luke 11:5–11, ***Then Jesus said to them, "Suppose one of you goes to his friend at midnight and says, 'Friend, lend me three loaves of bread, 6because a friend of mine has come to me on a journey, and I have nothing to set before him.' And suppose the one inside answers, 'Do not bother me. My door is already shut, and my children and I are in bed. I cannot get up to give you anything.' I tell you, even though he*** *will not get up to provide for him because of his friend-ship, yet because of the man's persistence, he will get up and give him as much as he needs. So I tell you: Ask, and it will be given to you; seek, and you will find; knock, and the door will be opened to you. For everyone who asks receives; he who seeks finds; and to him who knocks, the door will be opened. What father among you, if his son asks for a fish, will give him a snake instead? Or if he asks for an egg, will give him a scorpion? So if you who are evil know how to give good gifts to your children, how much more will your Father in heaven give the Holy Spirit to those who ask Him!"* (BSB)

The one who fails to offer a neighbor what they really need if they are able to spare it only cares for themselves. The parent that knows the truth and lies to their child does not love the child and the friend that lies is no friend. When we are able to recognize the failings in ourselves, we become better people. We are created in the image of יהוה, even the people who have never been exposed to His word are able to recognize it when they hear it. Some will reject it but those who accept it do so eagerly. Today with so much exposure to evil in our world we must continually be careful not to be trapped by what sounds too good to be true, we must not eat the fruit we are told to avoid. Instead we should remember to embrace the sacred word of our Creator and follow HIs instructions.

Many Christians would argue that Jesus came to abol-ish the law but no place in the Bible is that written. ישוע did come to challenge the man made rules of the Pharisees of his time and remind everyone that the Covenant would be renewed so that everyone would have the opportunity to be part of the family of יהוה. If we want to live in His kingdom, we must obey His rules and not our own man made rule we try to justify by twisting scripture. The choices we make today are quite simple, we can either reject יהוה and His instructions and rebel against Him, or we can accept His sacred word and embrace Him for who and what He is.

Deuteronomy 13:4, ***Ye shall walk after the Lord your God, and fear him, and keep his commandments, and obey his voice, and ye shall serve him, and cleave unto him.*** (KJV) Moses writes this just prior to giving the instructions for how to recognize a false prophet. He is reminding us to be careful who we listen to and be very careful who we choose to follow. Failure to listen for the voice of יהוה and to do obey His commands will cause you to be thrown into a lake of fire and be forever forgotten. You are given the freedom to choose that if you really want it, you can reject יהוה and be forgotten. Or, you can accept His word, live the way He designed you to live and be remembered forever.

The choice is given to each of us, reject the lies we have inherited and live or reject יהוה and die the second and final death. bow down to the idols or some false אלהים, or worship only יהוה. Now is the time to stop trying to justify your lifestyle, stop making excuses and be honest with yourself. When people have any kind of problem they tend not to want to resolve the issue that created the problem, they only want to cover the problem up so they can continue living the lifestyle that create the problem to begin with. יהוה is offering you the chance to solve the real problems, to shape you into the person He designed you to be. What will your choice be? accept Him or reject Him. The choice is yours but I encourage you to reject the lies and embrace the truth that is the sacred word of יהוה.

*You have been given the authority to reject they
lies you have inherited and rebuke the evil that
causes the chaos in your life.*

*You have the authority to embrace the truth
found in the sacred word of יהוה and inherit
His kingdom,*

Choose wisely.

The lies we have inherited from our fathers and the prayers to the אלהים that can not hear and will not answer appear to have given the enemies of יהוה a great amount of support. This illusion of strength will be the downfall of the adversary. He has convinced many people that good is evil and evil is good, but for the committed believer, we can trust the sacred word or יהוה. Then when all is finally completed, we can shout Hallelujah! יהוה wins!

May יהוה bless you and guard you,

May יהוה lift His eyes toward you and offer you an abundance of grace.

May the light of יהוה face shine brightly on you and remove all of the chaos that causes you unrest

(Jerry Mitchell translation)